Thumbs Up!

Thumbs Up!
The
Elizabeth Manley
Story

Elizabeth Manley
as told to Elva Clairmont Oglanby

Macmillan of Canada
A Division of Canada Publishing Corporation
Toronto, Ontario, Canada

Every effort has been made to identify and credit appropriately the sources of all photographs in this book. Any further information will be appreciated and acknowledged in subsequent editions.

Canadian Cataloguing in Publication Data
Manley, Elizabeth, 1965-
   Thumbs up

ISBN 0-7715-9101-2

1. Manley, Elizabeth, 1965- . 2. Skaters – Canada – Biography.
3. Women skaters – Canada – Biography. I. Oglanby, Elva
Clairmont. II. Title.
GV850.M36A3 1990   796.91'2'092   C90-094537-0

1 2 3 4 5   ARC   94 93 92 91 90

Cover design by Libby Starke
Cover photograph courtesy of the Edmonton Sun

Macmillan of Canada
A Division of Canada Publishing Corporation
Toronto, Ontario, Canada

Printed in the U.S.A.

To my mother, the sister and best friend I never had.
Through good and bad, sunshine and rain, there will always be us.
I love you with all my heart and dedicate my career to you.
Our road may have been bumpy,
but you always turned me in the right direction.

To my father, making up for lost time has been so wonderful
and I treasure every moment of it.
I may have grown up quickly,
but I will forever be your little girl.
I love you Daddy.

To my brothers, Tim, Tom, and Greg,
the most adorable, crazy men in my life.
You are my inspiration for everything I do.
I would be lost without you.

To Betty, with all my heart,
thank you for loving my father
and for all your support.

To Peter and Sonya,
there are no words special enough for you.
My night in Calgary was for you.
You've made my childhood dream come true.

To Michael and Nancy,
the real world would have been a nightmare
for me if you hadn't taken me in.
I'm honored to be with you and if this is all a dream
we are experiencing ... promise never to wake me up!

To all the children in the world:
to truly love something is success in itself.
That's what dreams are made of!

Thumbs Up!

Chapter One

I was born August 7, 1965, on a hot summer night in Belleville, Ontario. I came out kicking and hollering, which doesn't really surprise me because I've been that way ever since. For the first ten days of my life I was referred to as Diane Marie, but my Dad's lifelong passion for Elizabeth Taylor prevailed and I became Elizabeth Anne.

I was an army brat, the fourth child in the family and the first girl. I was fiercely competitive and wasted no time in my efforts to catch up to my brothers. Every once in a while they would allow me to win at something, just to keep the peace.

Only one of my grandparents is still living, Mom's father, Bruce Anderson. He is one of my closest friends and I visit him every chance I get. He lives in Deux-Montagnes in Quebec, where he was a bank manager until he retired. Mom's mother, Edna Celeste, was a sweet, gentle lady who spent the last seven years of her life bedridden. She died in 1981.

My Dad's father, Michael Joseph Manley, died when Dad was just two years old, so he was raised by his Mom, Catherine, and his stepfather. I have only a very faint memory of Catherine, because she died when I was barely five, but I have a feeling I would have liked her a lot, and she would have understood me.

Mom is very like her father — small, strong, determined, and with a will of iron. She was christened Joan, and I like to tease her that she was named after the saint because of all the burdens she's had to carry during her life. Not that she ever complains — she is always the optimist, finding ways to accomplish even the most impossible-seeming tasks. She used to be a talented athlete, but she was never really a competitor at heart. She much prefers sport as a recreational pastime.

Dad, on the other hand, is intensely competitive. He grew up playing all kinds of games and was extremely achievement-oriented in school. He is a strong believer in higher education and sees university as a indispensable stepping-stone to success. He was born Bernard Joseph, but no one ever calls him that. He is always referred to as Red, after the thatch of flame-colored hair that he passed on to us. He is an energetic man, with a powerful personality and an outstanding ability to organize. People rarely say no to Dad.

He joined the armed forces as a young man and made the army a career. He was always traveling while I was growing up, and I saw very little of him. I have vivid memories of waiting impatiently for him to return from some faraway place, laden with gifts for us all. As he came through the door, I would run screaming to greet him, hugging his knees and tugging at his jacket. He would always be filled with stories of his adventures, and we would listen enthralled as he spun tales of exotic lands like China, Japan, Africa, and India. Our house was decorated with artifacts from all over the world.

When I was five, we moved to Winnipeg for a year, and it was there that I had my first skating lesson. Mom drove us to a lake just outside the city one bitter winter afternoon. She had bought new skates for my youngest brother, Greg, so I had inherited his old ones. Mom tied them on for me, trying to lace them up quickly before her fingers froze. I felt right at home on the ice and skated around happily for half an hour, then I told Mom that the skates hurt my feet. "That's because you're not used to them," she said. It wasn't until we took them off that we discovered that they were on the wrong feet.

We moved to Trenton, Ontario, the next year and lived in a big yellow house with trees all around. I loved that house, and I remember it particularly well because is was one of the last times that our family would live all together. We were happy in those days, even though Dad continued to travel a great deal.

I used to pester my brothers to let me play street hockey with them. They, of course, were not crazy about my attempts to join in, but every so often they would set up a goal in the backyard, make me the goalie, and shoot pucks at me.

While we were in Trenton, I started first grade at Prince Charles Public School. I enjoyed schoolwork, and took part eagerly in all the activities, but even in those days I was finding it difficult to concentrate. Skating had already become my number-one priority.

By the time I was in third grade, I was skating every night. I took lessons from Howard Richardson, one of the resident coaches at the Trenton Figure Skating Club. About a dozen of us would have stroking classes twice a week. Stroking is the basic skating action that propels the skater either backward or forward along the ice surface. Mr. Richardson would stand by the boards, watching each of us as we stroked around the rink. "Stand up straight," he would shout. "Relax, keep your knees straight and your feet parallel. Make sure your weight is even on both feet. Look straight ahead, not down. Extend your arms away from your sides, hands at hip level, palms down. Make sure your shoulders are square to the direction you're moving in. Same with your hips." There were so many things to remember — I thought I would never get it right. Eventually, though, after hours and hours of practice, all these details became automatic.

Friday nights were special, something I longed for all week. Mom would pick me up right after school, buy me a hamburger, and then drive me to the rink for an unbroken four-hour session. At eight, when the public session started, she would drive me home again, make supper, and put me to bed. Then, after midnight, she would waken me and drive me back to the club.

The owner had taken a special liking to us and realized we couldn't afford to rent private ice, so every Friday night he let us have the whole rink to ourselves free of charge after one in the morning. We were allowed to stay as long as we liked; no one was there to bother us. I lived for these sessions, reveling in the great expanse of open ice and the freedom it gave me. I swooped and glided, improvising, experimenting, and practicing my jumps over and over again. Poor Mom sat up in the music booth, patiently knitting and changing tapes. I still don't know how she managed to stay awake.

Saturdays I could skate for only a short time, because most of the ice time during the day was devoted to hockey games. I stayed at the rink anyway, watching my brothers play and cheering them on. All three of them were first-class players.

Like me, my brothers were driven by a powerful will to succeed. My eldest brother, Tim, who is nine years older than me, is the most like Dad, and from the time he was very young he dreamed of following Dad into the armed forces. Tom, the middle brother, who is seven years older than me, has always been known as Radar, after the character in M.A.S.H. He has a fantastic instinct for business and an ability to juggle several aspects of his life without compromising any one of them. Greg, four years my senior, is the artistic one. As the youngest boy, I think he always felt the need to prove himself, and this tendency often landed him in hot water.

I remember the days in Trenton as being very happy. We had the usual childhood squabbles, of course, but we also had a lot of fun. We were always up to something, laughing and joking around, and Tim would think up complicated games for us to play. We were never bored, existing as we did in a little, tight-knit world of our own.

When he was thirteen, Tim decided he wanted his

own apartment. He was deadly serious about it and spent his time plotting how to achieve this goal. Money, of course, was a major problem — he had only thirty dollars saved up, which severely limited his choices. Eventually he left the house one morning before anyone else was up. There was a lot of commotion in the back-yard and a great deal of coming and going. The last things we heard were the sound of his mattress bump-ing down the stairs and the slamming of the back door. He had moved into the toolshed.

Tim considered this a perfectly acceptable residence. The shed was painted like a miniature house, with win-dows and roof tiles and flowers outside the door. Inside he had fixed it all up with a chair, a card table, his mattress, cushions, and a picnic cooler. He announced generously that he would be willing to continue eating meals with us so that we would have an opportunity to see him. He would also need to use our washing machine and bathroom until he could make arrange-ments to have his own plumbing installed. Mom and Dad kept straight faces, but Tom, Greg, and I thought the whole thing was hilarious and planted rubber snakes outside his door. He was in residence for three days until an unexpected cold spell caught him off-guard and drove him inside in the middle of the night. "Only for a day or two," he announced. "Just till I get my heating installed."

My father was always after Tom to get his hair cut, and one time when Dad came home after a trip, he caught sight of Tom and his friend Jeff talking in the street. They both had hair down their backs and cascading across their eyes like a curtain. Dad couldn't stand it any longer. He telephoned Jeff's father and told him to bring a pair of scissors and meet him outside in ten minutes.

As soon as they saw the scissors, Tom and Jeff knew what was about to happen. Dad yelled for them to stop, but they took off down the road at top speed, with Dad and Jeff's father in hot pursuit and half the kids in the neighborhood bringing up the rear. Mom called after us as we ran out the door to join in. Finally Dad caught them in someone's driveway, and he and Jeff's father held them down on the lawn while they chopped off the offending locks. Tim, Greg, and I stood looking over the fence, screaming with laughter and jumping up and down.

Dad was a relentless practical joker, and I was his most susceptible victim. I remember one April Fool's Day when he called me from the army base and told me to get out of the house quickly because it was on fire. I dropped the phone and started to scream, running across the road to a neighbor's house. "There's a fire in our house!" I howled. The neighbor was alarmed. "Elizabeth, calm down," she pleaded. "Where is it? What happened?" I explained through my tears that I didn't know where it was — that my Dad had just telephoned to tell me about it. When she heard this she marched me back across the road and handed me the telephone, which I had left dangling from the wall. Dad was still on the other end. "April Fool!" he chuckled.

When I was in the fourth grade, Tim and Tom went away to Toronto to live. They had become serious hockey players and had joined the Junior League. They went to school there and boarded in the city. I missed them a lot at first, but gradually I got used to it. Greg and I formed a strong love/hate relationship, and soon afterward we began to skate as a dance team. I'm not sure whose idea it was to put the two of us together, but it was an idea destined to fail.

I was eight years old at the time and enormously bossy. I always wanted to be in charge, to do things my way. I was also obsessed by the need to accomplish new technical moves on the ice. The problem was that I was slow to learn new moves — I needed to do things over and over again before I got the hang of them, and I needed three times as many lessons as anyone else. Greg, on the other hand, was the fastest learner I have ever seen. He had only to be shown something once and he could do it right away. He could do a spectacular Russian split jump, leaping into the air with both legs straight out to each side. I was wild with envy.

We were physically well-matched, Greg and I, with our red hair and blue eyes and almost identical physiques. We looked so cute together that it seemed we were a dance team made in heaven. Nothing could have been further from the truth, however. We fought ferociously every time we performed. We argued constantly, and we couldn't get once around the ice without my hitting him. I would stop right in the middle of a step and start punching, accusing him of doing everything wrong. We must have looked like a comedy act. Poor Greg, he always got the blame, but probably it was my fault most of the time. I had such a strong personality, and I was tough, opinionated, and determined — all things that worked in my favor as a singles skater. To an ice-dance team, though, they were fatal. Ice dance depends on perfect harmony and coordination between the partners, and we were always at war with each other.

In those days I even saw myself in competition with Mom. She bought us matching skating dresses, and we often skated sessions together. Mom had a natural talent, easily mastering things that took me forever to get the hang of. I would drive myself into a frenzy, trying to outdo her, but it was never any use. She was a better skater than I.

One terrible day we were doing side-by-side sit spins. I had learned to do them in my weekly classes and had progressed from doing them on both feet to doing them on one foot. You start from a standing spin and then drop into a sitting position with one leg thrust forward. I was concentrating extra hard, trying to impress Mom, when I heard a scream. Mom's blade had caught in a rut, stopping her spin cold, but the momentum had forced her body to keep on turning. She was lying on the ice, writhing in pain.

Her leg was broken in three places, and she had to stay in the hospital overnight. Since Dad was away at the time, a neighbor came in to take care of Greg and me. I was inconsolable, feeling it had somehow been my fault. I was convinced Mom was going to die, and I lay in her bed, crying hysterically all night and begging God to bring her back. She spent weeks on crutches and even after the leg had fully healed, she was too terrified to put skates on again. Her skating days were over.

My first coach was a man called Dwight Carpenter. When I went to the rink to meet him, he asked me to show him everything I had learned so far. He stood at the boards watching me carefully. After a while, he pulled me over to the side.

"Have you been having trouble with spins?" he asked.

I nodded. "I just can't seem to get them right."

He smiled at me. "I'm not a bit surprised. You've been jumping one way and spinning the other. Every skater has a natural way of turning, either clockwise or anti-clockwise, but you've been doing things both ways. You jump to the left and spin to the right. Your jumps are fine, but since you seem to be having such difficulty with the spins, I would guess your natural rotation is to the left." He paused, to see if I was following him. "Let's start over, and try spinning to the left."

I did as he suggested and to my amazement, I found that he was right. As I grew accustomed to the new direction, I became more and more confident, until I could spin as easily and surely as I jumped.

"Excellent, Elizabeth," Mr. Carpenter told me. "I thought that must be the problem. You were spinning against your natural inclination. It's like making a left-handed person write with his right hand — it's disorienting."

Mr. Carpenter was always suggesting to Mom that I should be more independent. One day, toward the end of my session, I had to leave the ice to go to the bathroom, which was off the lobby. I had to push my way through throngs of hockey players waiting to follow me on the ice, and when I came out I called for Mom to come and refasten my skating dress. Mr. Carpenter, who was talking to her, put his hand on her arm. "She's quite old enough to fasten her own skating dress by now," he said loudly, and I felt everyone in the lobby turn to look at me. I was horribly embarrassed. I dived back into the bathroom and hid there until I heard the hockey players banging through the swing doors leading to the rink. From then on, I always insisted on doing everything for myself.

Around this time I was introduced to school figures. We did these on a clean patch of ice and skated in prescribed patterns, tracing circles, loops, figures of eight, and similar curved shapes in various combinations. There are nineteen different figures to be learned. We had to do them not only on either foot, but on each edge of the blade for each foot, and traveling either forward or backward. Once the original figure had been laid out, we had to skate over our own tracings without deviating from the lines. They have to be done very slowly and smoothly as an exercise in control and accuracy. It took a long time to do each patch and required intense concentration, which I always found a strain.

❄

When I was nine, I changed coaches. Beth Post was a skilled teacher — tough, demanding, and unyielding. This often clashed with my determination to do things my own way and in my own time, and she must have found me a difficult student to work with. I know there were times when my failure to follow her instructions drove her to distraction.

One Thursday night, she was trying to teach me the right way to land a double loop jump. You enter this jump while traveling backward, do two full turns in the air, and continue moving backward when you land. I did it over and over, but still Beth wasn't satisfied. "Elizabeth," she said with exaggerated patience, "you'll never be able to land this jump until you get the body position right. Sometimes I think you're doing this wrong on purpose." I tried one more time, but fell heavily on the ice. As I was struggling to pick myself up, I saw my skate guards flying out across the ice toward me. Beth had hurled them out of sheer frustration.

She came across to me then, and stood looking at me with her hands on her hips and her head tilted to one side. Finally she drew a deep breath. "Elizabeth, we seem to be locked in some kind of battle of wills, but we're going to have to come to an understanding if you're ever going to make progress." She paused for a moment. "You do *want* to learn, don't you?"

I nodded. "Yes," I whispered.

"I thought so. All right, let's start again, and this time, listen to what I say. Pay attention. Trust me, okay?" Beth skated back to the side of the rink and turned to face me. "Now let's try it my way!"

I did as she asked, and the jump was definitely better. I managed to hold on to the landing edge, and felt much more secure, even though I continued to have trouble with the take-off.

I worked with Beth for another year and ultimately mastered a passable double loop. That year she took me away to my first summer school, in Oshawa. I looked forward to it, anticipating the fun I was going to have, but when it actually arrived, it wasn't quite the way I'd imagined it.

I boarded with one of the local skating families, and

they tried hard to make me welcome. The trouble was that I had never been away from home before and I was homesick. I missed Mom and Dad, Greg, my house, and my friends. Sometimes, when I was in bed at night with the light out, I cried into my pillow. I tried hard not to make a noise, because I didn't want anyone to know I was unhappy.

As the summer progressed, however, I began to enjoy myself more. For one thing, I was learning all the time. Among other things, I mastered a double salchow, which I had always thought was the most beautiful of the jumps. It is named after its inventor, Ulrich Salchow. You enter it while traveling backward, taking off from the inside back edge of one skate, rotating twice in the air, and landing on the outside back edge of the other skate.

We also worked hard at freestyle movement, learning how to enter jumps and spins not only correctly, but gracefully, so that the connections from one element to another flowed smoothly. And we learned ways of making the footwork between our jumps and spins interesting and creative.

I made friends with some of the other students and we would go on picnics together, or to parties given by the host families. We were there for six weeks and when the time came to go home, I was actually reluctant to leave. I didn't want to say goodbye to my new friends.

Beth was pleased with the progress I had made at summer school, and the clashes between us became less frequent. I had learned to trust her and although I was still in awe of her, I felt much more comfortable during our sessions together.

❄

I skated in a number of competitions that year, but the first one I really remember well is the Canadian Armed Forces Figure Skating Competition at Camp Borden, Ontario, in April 1975. Mom bought me a new skating dress for the occasion, because I was entered in three events and I had only two outfits. My new dress was my favorite — a white beaded bodice with a skirt made of flame-colored petals. I felt very sophisticated in it.

I was taking part in the Junior Dance competition with Tim Klemencic, the brother of my best friend, Barbara. The three of us traveled down to Camp Borden in Mom's car and made so much noise it was a wonder she didn't drive right off the road. I was almost hysterical with excitement and couldn't wait to get out on the ice.

Tim and I took the gold medal in the Junior Dance and got a standing ovation at the end of our program. I think it must have been because we were so tiny, dressed in little red plaid outfits. We had made up a program using Scottish music and movements from reels and jigs. I also took gold medals in the Junior Ladies Open and the Juvenile Ladies, so I had a real bonanza at that competition.

In the summer of 1975, when I was nine, Dad received word that he was to be transferred to Ottawa. I had mixed feelings about the move. I had so many close friends in Trenton, and it wouldn't be easy to leave them behind. Trenton was a small town, a warm, close-knit community, where you could walk around the streets and always meet someone you knew. Everything was familiar and comfortable and made you feel safe. On the other hand, the idea of going to the city was exciting. Once I had accepted it I began to look forward to the prospect.

Mom and I moved first so that I could skate in a summer school at the Gloucester Figure Skating Club. Greg stayed behind with Dad and helped to pack up the house. I had an odd feeling of euphoria inside me as Mom and I entered the Gloucester arena for the first time, as if something momentous was about to happen. It was then that I met the man who was to be my coach for the next seven years and who was to bring me into the competitive skating world.

Chapter Two

Bob McAvoy was a wonderfully enthusiastic coach who made everything seem like an adventure to me. I loved him from the moment I met him, and I could sense that he liked working with me. We established a good rapport immediately, which filled me with new confidence. He had had a successful skating career of his own before turning professional, and had competed at the World Championships in 1969 in the pairs event.

Toward the end of the summer school, Bob told me that he would like to continue working with me. "Not as a casual thing," he said, "but as a total commitment. You have everything it takes to become a champion, Elizabeth, and if you're ready for years of hard work, then I believe you can realize that potential. But you have to understand, it doesn't happen overnight."

I listened to what he was saying, my heart hammering against my ribs. I knew I wanted this more than anything in the world, but I wasn't sure what Mom and Dad were going to say about it.

"Go home and talk it over with your folks," Bob said. "It isn't just a question of your own commitment. If this is to happen, then it will take a great deal of time and effort on their part, and a major financial sacrifice. They have to think carefully about that."

He walked me to the door and put a hand on my shoulder. "I believe in you, Elizabeth," he said. "I just want you to know that if you decide to do this, I'll be there for you all the way through."

I was so excited by the time I got home that I couldn't eat. Mom knew something was up. "Why don't you tell me what's bothering you, Elizabeth?" she asked. I told her what Bob had suggested, my words spilling out in a breathless rush. Mom always weighed the pros and cons of a situation before coming to any decision, so I didn't expect to have an answer right away. But I had no sooner finished than she said, "All right, Elizabeth. If it's what you want, then I think we should do it."

I jumped on her and hugged her so hard that she gasped. "Mom, I love you, I love you," I squealed.

She smiled. "I just hope you remember that when the going gets tough," she said.

❄

I started to train eighteen hours a week, and Mom took a job at the Department of Transport to help pay the increased costs. It was very hard on Dad and Greg, because they rarely saw her — she would drive me to the rink before she left for work in the morning and again when she finished at five. Dad did most of the cooking, and Greg pitched in to help with the dishes and the cleaning.

As for me, all the training meant that I could no longer take part in school sports, which I had always enjoyed. I had done track and field, and was good at short-distance running, and I'd also taken gymnastics for a while, but eighteen hours of skating a week pretty well preempted any other kind of sports involvement. I often used to wish there were more hours in the day!

In Bob McAvoy I had found a coach who really seemed to understand me. He was gentle and patient, but he also had an authority that I rarely questioned. Under his careful tutoring I began to shed my fears, and he encouraged me to listen to music and integrate it into my skating. "You have to feel it, Elizabeth," he would say. "Ride it. You can't use it as a backdrop, it has to be part of everything you do."

Technically, I improved steadily. I learned to be innovative within the context of solid technique, and I had a new level of confidence that amazed my family.

I began to pass the tests required to move up the ladder toward serious competitive skating, earning one gold medal after another. Inside, I felt the first stirrings of ambition, and I was as happy as I had ever been in my life.

Greg, by this time, had quit skating. Our ice dance sessions had mercifully been terminated long before, no doubt because it had become a real possibility that we might do each other a serious injury. He had tried singles skating for a while, proving to be an extraordinarily gifted and creative student. He was definitely a candidate for future gold medals, but he was also trying hard to relate to his new group of friends, none of whom considered skating to be a suitable pastime for a "real man." Under the weight of this persistent peer pressure, he finally gave up. We'll never know how far he might have gone had he continued.

❄

From the time we moved to Ottawa, my parents began to grow apart. It didn't happen overnight, and it wasn't anything dramatic, but their marriage gradually eroded to the point of no return. They were careful to shield us from the fallout, trying hard not to allow the inevitable bitterness to affect us.

I had been so busy skating that I hardly noticed what was happening. I knew Mom was unhappy, but thought it was because of the new environment. I thought she didn't like living in Ottawa. I would often come home from school and find her with red, swollen eyes, but she would claim to be suffering from a cold, or from hay fever. She always managed to pull herself together in front of Greg and me, and on the surface our lives were much the same as usual. Dad was often away, of course, so we rarely witnessed the friction that had developed between them.

Tim and Tom were still living on their own, following the hockey circuit, and they only came home for summer vacations. As our second summer in Ottawa approached, Greg and I began to anticipate the day when they would return. At the beginning of June I asked Mom when they were due to arrive, and she looked at me sadly and told me to go and get Greg. "I have something to tell you both," she said quietly.

Mom explained to us that she and Dad hadn't been getting along and that they had decided to live apart. It had nothing to do with us and it wasn't anyone's fault — it was just something that sometimes happened to married people. I stared at her in disbelief, trying to take it in.

"Where will we go?" I asked. "Why can't Dad live with us anymore?" I wasn't prepared for the speed with which this was all happening.

"Dad will keep this house," Mom said, "and I will find an apartment somewhere near here. That way, whichever home you choose to live in, it won't be far away from the other one." She paused, looking at us for a moment. Then she said, "Whatever happens, you mustn't ever think any of this is something you could have prevented. Dad and I love you both very, very much."

Mom moved to an apartment complex in Gloucester, a suburb of Ottawa. Money was tight, so she could afford only a very small place, but it had the advantage of being near the skating club. I chose to live with her — I couldn't imagine anything else, because she was so much a part of my life. Greg opted to stay in Ottawa with Dad, but I saw him frequently, and after a while we got used to the new arrangement. Tim and Tom stayed in Toronto and rarely came back to visit. This was the saddest part of the whole situation for me, because over the months we began to grow apart.

By the time the new skating season came around, I was over the initial shock. One of the ladies at the

Gloucester Figure Skating Club, Marilyn Dunwoodie, came forward during this period to help Mom get back on her feet. She knew money was a problem and tried to get free ice time for me whenever it was needed. This meant a significant saving for us, since ice time cost about $60 an hour. She also made an effort to involve us in her own social circle, and she often invited us for dinner at her house. Her encouragement, coming as it did at a time when I was just beginning the long climb up the ladder, acted as a tremendous motivating force.

❋

I had been entering competitions since the age of five, when I had placed fifth in the Cobourg Inter-Club Competition in 1971, and I had won several gold medals along the way. In 1974, however, I took part in the first event in which I was able to compete against really good skaters. This was the Palestre Nationale in Montreal, and I finished in third place behind the local champion, Charlene Wong. I have always been stimulated by being pitted against really tough opponents, and Charlene — besides being my fifth cousin — is one of the toughest opponents I've ever encountered. I wanted desperately to beat her, and after three years I finally made it, winning the Palestre Nationale in 1976. I was beside myself with excitement at that. Charlene and I formed a lasting friendship and to this day she is still one of the skaters I most admire.

In 1975, just before I left Trenton, I had entered the Eastern Ontario Sectionals in Ottawa, competing in the Juvenile Ladies division. It was a big thing for me, because Sectionals are the first stepping-stone toward the national level. I was only ten, but I already had big dreams of being a champion, and I was intensely competitive — the bigger the challenge, the better I liked it. The Trenton Figure Skating Club was very supportive of me; they had never produced a medal winner before and saw in me the potential they sought. Many of them came to Ottawa to cheer me on, and when I ended up winning the gold medal, there was tremendous excitement. They threw a celebratory party for my whole family.

When I moved to the Gloucester club in late 1975, I took part in all the local competitions, entering both Ladies and Ice Dance events. (Each competition has four categories: single ladies, single men, ice dancing, and pairs. In pairs skating, the skaters are allowed all sorts of overhead lifts, throws, and side-by-side maneuvers. In ice dancing, the skaters are not allowed to separate for more than a few seconds at a time, nor are they allowed to lift above the waist.) At this point in my career, I relished the variety, and I was one of the few singles skaters who had passed all the gold ice-dance tests. Bob encouraged me, urging me to get as much experience as I could before the time came for me to specialize. He also broadened my cultural horizons, bringing me books and tapes and taking me to see visiting dance companies. He encouraged me to study dance myself, so I took a ballet class once a week after school, and a jazz class on Saturdays. I was the youngest person in the jazz class, everyone else was an adult, but I loved those classes. As for the ballet, it taught me a lot about posture and grace, developing the upper body, so often neglected by skaters. I eventually had to give it up, however, because the teacher told us that if I planned to continue, I would have to get toe shoes and start pointe work. This would have put the wrong kind of strain on my feet, so I decided to stop taking ballet.

All these classes stood me in good stead in my favorite event of all, the Interpretive Dance Competition, in which the skater goes out during the pre-competition warm-up period and hears a piece of music for the first time. The music is repeated three times in a row, then the ice is cleared and the skaters are given a skating order. When your turn comes to skate, you have to go out and interpret the music you've just heard, making up choreography as you go along. I loved this, much preferring the freedom it gave me over the more restrictive requirements of the prechoreographed programs. I learned so much about music from these events, about how to feel it and how to react to it, that I lost all my inhibitions in the process. Later in my career, this stood me in good stead, giving me more confidence when it came to selecting music for my competitive programs, and encouraging a sense of adventure that gave me a certain creative edge.

Bob had become like a father to me since my parents' separation. He sensed my turmoil over the impending divorce and tried to keep me busy, distracting me with an exhausting schedule. I would wake up early every day and skate for three hours (two patches of figures and one free-skating session), then shower and go to school, study during my lunch break, go back to the rink again right after school, and work until seven at night. Then I would go home, shower again, eat supper, and study until it was time to go to bed. I never had any problem falling asleep.

❄

Bob had been trying for some time to teach me to land a good double axel. The axel is one of the hardest jumps to do, since it actually involves an extra half revolution and is the only jump entered while the skater is traveling forward. I would attempt one after the other, but always to no avail. I just couldn't seem to get it right, no matter what I did. Bob racked his brain, trying to think of some way to bribe me, and eventually discovered my passion for skating pins. He had a jacket covered in pins, some dating back as far as the early fifties. "All right, Elizabeth," he said one day. "The first time you land a great double axel, you get to choose any pin you want." It was all the incentive I needed. I worked like a fiend, and within the week I was landing them consistently and was the proud owner of a pin from the 1964 Olympic Games. Later I added another, a reward for landing my first triple toe loop, so called because you use the toe pick of the skate blade to take off and do three full turns in the air.

I was still taking both dance and singles simultaneously and moving steadily through the various tests conducted by the Canadian Figure Skating Association. There are nine of them in each category, beginning with a preliminary test and ending with the Gold test. Beyond that level is the Senior Competitive Test, which involves both figures and free skating. Each test is judged according to the degree of technical difficulty involved and the skill with which the skater performs. Bob's reward for passing each test was a ten-dollar bill, and this proved to be the most powerful bribe of all. Mom couldn't afford to give me an allowance at that time, so I had never had any money of my own. I passed test after test, and eventually took the Gold test in both single skating and ice dancing, earning more than one hundred dollars in all.

Mom was having a difficult time coping with things and Grandpa sent us tickets to Quebec so we could visit them during the Easter vacation. Greg came with us, and we were a happy gathering, enjoying the warmth and security of my grandparents' home. Grandma had been seriously ill for some years and was permanently bedridden, but she hadn't lost her interest in life around her. I spent hours sitting by her bed, playing games with her and telling her about the world of skating. We looked through old photo albums, and she would point out pictures of Mom as a young girl and tell me how much I looked like her. One evening, just as I was leaning down to kiss her good night, she pulled me closer. "Look after your Mom, Elizabeth," she said softly. "She needs you now." I hugged her and promised I would do my best.

Chapter Three

All through November 1977, I worked with feverish concentration, preparing for the Novice Ladies event in the Eastern Ontario Sectionals in Trenton.

Just before we left for the competition, in early December, we decided to run through my numbers back to back. It was a Thursday evening, and Mom was watching from the stands. We started with the short program. (This is a routine of about one and a half to two minutes, during which the competitor must perform seven elements — jumps and spins — that have been set ahead of time by the judges. The competitor chooses the music and arranges the choreography, but those seven elements are compulsory.) I did my short program smoothly, without a hitch. "Good," said Bob. "Now let's try the long program — remember to watch your entry into the double salchow."

The music started and I moved easily through the first minute and a half of my four-minute routine. I felt fine. I prepared for the double salchow, judging the exact moment to take off, checking to make sure I wouldn't be too close to the boards. As I left the ice I felt my center of balance shift. A split second later I lost control and fell heavily.

Bob hurried across to me, but when he tried to help me up, a sharp pain tore through my back. I screamed. It felt as though my back was on fire. "I can't move my head," I whispered.

Mom phoned for an ambulance and a half hour later I was in the emergency room of the Ottawa Civic Hospital being examined by a doctor. He X-rayed me and asked a million questions, prodding up and down my spine and taking notes. Finally, to our relief, he announced that nothing was broken. "You've got whiplash," he told me. "It's painful, but if you wear a neck brace it won't feel quite so bad."

"What about skating?" I asked. "Can I skate?"

The doctor looked at me strangely, then he turned to Mom and Bob. "If you feel it's absolutely necessary, she can continue to practice, but she'll have to keep the neck brace on. However. . ." he paused for a moment to emphasize the point, ". . .if she falls again, before this injury has healed, she's liable to do some serious damage."

We talked it over and decided I could continue with school figures and do some restricted free skating practice, so I could at least keep in shape. The Sectionals were less than a week away, but the doctor thought I could take the brace off in five days. That would give me two days to rehearse my programs before the actual competitions.

When the brace came off, I felt lighter, freer. I tried gingerly to move my head, and found I could turn it all the way to the right and part of the way to the left. "Don't force it," warned the doctor. "It will adjust on its own if you give it time."

It felt awkward at first, jumping with the restricted movement, but I got used to it. Each time I skated, the muscles seemed to be a little more flexible.

On December 7, I competed in the Novice Ladies event in the Eastern Ontario Sectionals in Trenton — and won. Bob was ecstatic, because it qualified me to move into the Divisionals in Peterborough, the final competitive phase before the Nationals.

I had been experiencing quite a lot of difficulty with the Novice level for the previous two years. My figures were weak, and in the Novice events there was only one freestyle segment in which to pull up, so that I rarely managed to overcome my initial poor showing in the compulsory figures enough to win a medal. I was determined to do better at the Divisionals in Peterborough, but my neck was still stiff and even though I skated my heart out in the freestyle, I finished in seventh place and was out of the medals once again. I was terribly depressed about it.

The day after I got back to Gloucester, I went to my early-morning session with a heavy heart, sure I was never going to get past the Novice level. I seemed to have hit a roadblock. As I finished running though my program for the second time, I heard the sound of someone applauding and noticed one of the arena staff leaning over the boards. I skated over to him, and he held out his hand. "Bob McIsaac," he said, smiling. "I love to watch you skate. I hope you don't mind." I assured him that it actually helped me to have an audience, and he asked if I would show him some of my other programs. When the session was over, we sat in the lobby and chatted. He told me that he was nineteen and that he was working at the arena to pay his way through college. He wanted to be a pharmacist, like his father. I liked him immediately and we soon became good friends.

Bob McAvoy made a decision at this time in a desperate attempt to mobilize my progress. He took me out of the Novice level and moved me straight into the Junior category. Although the standards are higher at that level and the overall requirements are harder, I found myself performing much better because of the increased emphasis on free skating.

I had begun to get a small amount of money from the Skaters' Development Fund of the Canadian Figure Skating Association, which helped to cover my skating expenses, but they could only give a limited amount to each skater, and we still had trouble making ends meet. Bob was aware of the difficult time Mom was having financially, and he often gave me free lessons and refused to take any money for transporting me between rinks, which he did almost every day in the constant search for extra ice time. But there were all the other expenses — some big, some small. Skating is not an easy sport to pursue for those without much money, when you consider the fees for lessons and ice time; travel and accommodations during competitions; custom-made boots at several hundred dollars a pair; costumes; music tapes. . . the list goes on and on. And the more successful you get, the longer it grows.

I came home one Friday after school and found Mom sitting at the kitchen table, surrounded by piles of bills. As I walked through the door I saw that she had her head in the hands, and when she looked up I saw the tears trickling down her face. It wasn't like Mom to cry. She was one of the strongest people in the whole world and was always the one to offer reassurance to others. I ran over and put my arms around her. "Oh, Elizabeth," she said. "I just don't know how we're going to manage. I've got more bills than I've got paychecks."

I couldn't concentrate on my homework that evening. I wondered if this struggle was worth it — whether I should give up this ambition and put a stop to the whole escalating business. I couldn't bear to see Mom under such pressure, especially since I wasn't able to do anything to help her. I went down to supper, determined to quit.

In the kitchen, Mom was her old cheerful self again, all traces of the earlier despair completely gone. She was humming to herself as she fried sausages and eggs and poured boiling water into the teapot.

"It's okay, I solved the problem," she said happily. "I worked something out."

I sat at the table. "Mom," I said, "I think I should give up skating."

She whirled around in horror, her spatula dripping grease all over the floor. "After all this?" she said. "Just because of a couple of dollars? No way, Elizabeth. I'll manage. I've just had a bad day, that's all."

One morning at the rink, Bob introduced me to a lady named Anne Schelter. Anne was his partner — she did the choreography for many of his students and she produced and directed figure skating shows. She was an attractive and very talented person. She sat down with me and told me that she wanted to make up some new programs for me, but she wanted me to feel free to contribute my own ideas. "I've been watching you, Elizabeth," she said. "I believe I have a feel for what will look good on you. After this session, I'd like you to listen to some music I think you might enjoy."

I became increasingly agitated during the session, and after a while Bob pulled me over to the side. "What on earth is the matter, Elizabeth?" he asked. "Is something bothering you?"

I took a deep breath. I had to say something now before it was too late.

"I can't let Anne do any programs for me," I said firmly. "It's the money. Mom is just about broke as it is, and she can't possibly take on anything else."

Bob put his arm around me. He looked at me kindly and smiled. "Now I understand," he said. "But you don't have to worry about that. Anne isn't going to charge you anything for these programs — she just wants to work with you." I felt a wave of relief wash over me. Bob's generosity and belief in me, and now Anne's, made all the difference. I don't know how we would have managed without their help.

We started to develop a program to the music of Prokofiev's "Cinderella." It was a wonderful experience for me, working with a choreographer for the first time. Some choreographers make up the steps first and then find music to fit; others start with a piece of music and create movements to complement it. Anne worked the latter way, and she taught me a lot about listening to music. She was a very creative person, but she welcomed my ideas, encouraging me to contribute. Sometimes I would take one of her suggestions and extend or modify it in some way as I tried it out, and she would watch intently, weighing up the results. If she liked it, she would smile broadly and say, "Let's keep it." I was amazed at how many different moves we came up with between us.

Sometimes Bob McIsaac watched us from the side, leaning over the boards, shouting comments, and making us laugh. I had nicknamed him Rink Rat, and we always enjoyed his banter. It was difficult to be completely serious when he was around.

Bob McAvoy had taken on another student who quickly became a good friend of mine. Jean-Pierre Martin was almost the same age as me, and he was the strongest jumper I had ever seen. Bob knew that I was at my best when challenged, so he would often have the two of us skate together. We would throw off jumps in rapid succession, each trying to outdo the other. It was like World War III out there on the ice.

Off the ice, Jean-Pierre and I got along fantastically well. We spent hours together, riding in Bob's car, driving back and forth between practice sessions. He had a wonderful sense of humor and I found him very funny.

The World Championships were held in Ottawa in the spring of 1978, and I was chosen to be one of the flower girls. Mom was also working at the event, helping with the planning and the organization.

I was measured for my official outfit, and shown how to pick up the flowers thrown on to the ice by the spectators and hand them to the competitors. I felt very important as I waited by the barriers for each skater to finish, poised to skate out and scoop up armfuls of roses and carnations. I remember handing a bouquet to Robin Cousins, the British skater who went on to win the 1980 Olympic gold medal. He was a particular hero of mine, and he leaned over and kissed my cheek as he took the flowers. Little did I dream that I would one day make a television special with him!

Mom rode the official bus to the arena each day, and became friendly with the Russian team. She shared their wild sense of humor, and Igor Bobrin, the Russian men's champion, found her so much fun that he escorted her to the closing banquet, and taught her to drink Russian vodka.

❄

In the winter of 1978, Dad was transferred to Germany with the armed forces. One weekend, when Greg was visiting, he told me that he had decided to go with Dad. I was devastated at the thought of losing him. Things hadn't seemed so bad as long as he was around, and somewhere in the back of my mind I had held on to the hope that someday we would all live together again. Now I was faced with the prospect of losing not only Dad, but Greg as well. I cried for days, hoping against hope that he would change his mind at the last minute, but in the end I had to accept it. All my brothers were gone.

I missed Dad's being in Ottawa. Not that he had been around that often, but it was just the thought that he lived nearby that was important. It felt strange, not knowing what his home looked like now.

Not very long after he left, he phoned to say that his army base wanted me to come over and take part in a skating exhibition they were having. I was so excited I couldn't sleep.

The following Friday afternoon, I got permission to leave school early so Mom could drive me to the air base. I was to fly over on an armed forces jet that would arrive in Germany on Saturday morning. I was exhausted by the time the plane took off and before long I was fast asleep. When I woke up, the plane was about to begin its descent, and I could see the odd-shaped fields and pastures far below me, spread across the countryside like a crazy patchwork quilt.

Dad and Greg met me at the airport, and I hugged them hard. We had a mammoth breakfast in a small Tyrolean-style restaurant, and then Dad drove us back to his house at the army base in Lahr. I craned my neck this way and that, taking in all the sights. I asked endless questions and tried to learn a few words of German. In the afternoon I went to the rink to practice. There were almost a hundred soldiers sitting around in the bleachers, watching, and I put on a little show for them. Then I went back to Dad's place to rest.

The show was on Saturday evening, and I skated two numbers, one to music from Charlie Chaplin films, the other to an extract from *Swan Lake*. The response was terrific and very encouraging. Afterward, I showered and changed, and we all went to a huge reception given in honor of the skaters. Everyone was friendly and very complimentary. I slept soundly that night and woke up late on Sunday morning. I just had time for a quick breakfast before I had to go back to the air base to catch the plane for Canada.

When I arrived at school on Monday morning, slightly tired but none the worse for my experience, one of my friends asked me what I had done over the weekend. "I flew to Germany," I announced grandly. Several pairs of eyes turned to stare at me skeptically. "Yeah, sure," said my friend. "A likely story!"

❄

I competed in the Eastern Ontario Sectionals at the Junior level in Cornwall in December 1978 and finished third. Bob was pleased and told me I had done very well for my first time out. The Divisionals were in St. Laurent a month later, but there I managed only sixth place. I was terribly disappointed, feeling I had let everyone down, but Bob told me I had done much better than he had expected and that I should be pleased. "Be patient, Elizabeth," he said. "Remember what I told you? It isn't going to happen overnight."

Since we were already in Quebec, we went to visit my grandparents in Deux-Montagnes. Grandma was very frail and not really able to do things for herself any longer. As always, I sat with her and told her about what I had been doing, and she held on to my hand. Mom made light of her own situation, fending off questions about her finances and generally painting a rosy picture. She did such a good job she almost fooled herself.

When we got back to Ottawa, we realized that something had gone wrong for Bob at the Gloucester club. I didn't know the details, but I could sense the tension. He became increasingly dissatisfied, until one day in 1979 he told me that we were going to move to the Minto Club in Ottawa, and that Anne was coming too. It all happened so quickly that we didn't have time to dwell on it. I was sad at having to say goodbye to Bob McIsaac, whose cheerful chatter had kept us all entertained through many long, cold winter mornings, and to Jean-Pierre, who had been such a tremendous inspiration to me.

Mom went to my school for a conference with my teachers. She wanted them to work out a curriculum that would accommodate my heavy skating schedule. They were very supportive and they placed me on a semester system. I was to tackle my most difficult subjects — French and geography — first, and do the easier ones after Christmas, during the competition season. Mom was taking a government French-language training course, so we were able to practice our French conversation over dinner and in the car.

At the Minto Club, Bob started to work with a very good skater called Campbell Sinclair. He was already a regular contender at the national level and was a superb technician on the ice, with remarkable figures and jumps. Having him around, as I'm sure Bob knew only too well, proved to be an irresistible challenge to me. I worked extra hard, trying to beat him, stretching myself to my limits. Campbell and I became good friends — we both attended Woodroffe High School and spent hours driving to and from practice together. Although we didn't skate as a pair, he was in every other sense my skating partner.

Figures continued to be my nemesis. I was plagued by an inability to concentrate on the intricate tracings I was doing on the ice. For one thing, I was so small and light that my tracings were very faint and hard to see. I often found my mind wandering and I would sometimes even start absent-mindedly free skating on my patch of ice.

The idea behind school figures is to train the skater to perform exacting, complicated maneuvers with complete control and consistency. Circular diagrams are drawn on the ice with a scribe — a sort of giant metal compass. The skater then has to trace over these diagrams taking great care to follow the original lines exactly, without wobbling and without putting the free foot down on the ice. I found the whole exercise intensely boring, and would invent distractions for myself, just waiting for the session to end so I could do free skating again.

One morning I saw Campbell watching me. Eventually he came over to me. "What are you doing, Elizabeth?" he asked. "You keep jumping over your scribe." I blushed, because he was right. I had been pretending I was in a steeplechase.

"You have to learn to shut everything else out," he said. "You can't make your mind a blank, or else it will wander. You have to actually think about the figure you're tracing. Focus on it — watch every inch of it and control what you are doing."

I tried hard to do as he suggested, and I did improve a bit under his influence. It was difficult not to be affected by his uncanny ability to fix his attention on whatever he was doing, whether it was lacing up his boots or executing school figures. He was extremely self-disciplined, and it showed in his skating.

I competed in the Eastern Ontario Sectionals in November 1979 in Pembroke, and not only won the gold medal in the Junior Ladies division, but also made a little piece of skating history.

I had planned a triple combination jump for my short program — a triple salchow followed by a double loop — and Bob didn't really expect me to pull it off. No one had ever landed a triple combination in the history of Canadian Ladies competition before, however, and I wanted to be the first. I was in fourth place after compulsory figures, and even a series of falls during my warm-up didn't dampen my determination. I was burning to start.

I attacked the combination jumps with every ounce of energy I had, judging them carefully and concentrating furiously. I managed to land them both, and the audience was so shocked that everyone leapt up and began to scream. I had to fight hard to focus on the remaining two minutes in the program. The long program the next night was clean, and I became the Junior Ladies champion.

My performance in Pembroke caught the attention of the press and they began to write about me. It was all very exciting, and I went to the Divisional championships in Markham with high hopes. Again I won the gold medal. Suddenly I realized I would be going to the National Championships for the first time. I was beside myself with excitement, hardly able to eat or sleep. I had dreamed of this for so long.

Bob tried hard to keep me calm as we prepared to leave for Kitchener. Inside he was probably as tense as I was, but he didn't show it. Mom kept herself busy, making all the arrangements, finishing a new costume for me in blue-and-white layers. I tried hard not to think about the competition as Campbell and I ran through our programs and practiced our figures over and over again. "I'm going to go mad if I have to trace one more circle," I complained, but we had to keep going.

Finally the competitions started, and I surprised everybody by placing in the top three in compulsory figures. Bob couldn't believe it, but I knew it was partly due to the hours I had spent working with Campbell. I did well in the short program too, repeating my triple combination, and managed to hold on to third position.

Just before I went out onto the ice for the long program, Bob told me to go for it. "You have nothing to lose, Elizabeth," he said. "Just go out there and have fun."

I did exactly that, flying across the ice and landing every one of my jumps. As I finished my final scratch spin, I could hear the audience cheering and then I saw that all the people were on their feet. I had pulled up one more place to win a silver medal in my very first National championship.

Chapter Four

Back in Ottawa I had to concentrate on completing grade nine. It was hard, after the excitement of the Nationals, but I had lost a great deal of school time during the competitive season and I wanted to catch up. I was invited to skate a number of local exhibitions, and at the rink I continued to work out new programs.

The Canadian Figure Skating Association had started to take a greater interest in my career. Barbara Graham, the technical director of the association, told Bob that I could move straight into the Senior Ladies category and invited me to represent Canada in the Coupe des Alpes, a double-pronged competition to be held in August 1980. The first week would be in St. Gervais, France, and the second week in Oberstdorf, Germany. It would be my first international competition, and I would be skating as a Senior for the first time. I could hardly take it all in. Everything was happening so quickly — in two short years I had gone from a failing Novice to a world-level competitor.

❄

Ever since I had started at Woodroffe High School I had been pursued relentlessly by a boy named Rob Forcier. I had no real interest in dating him, and finally, having run out of tactful excuses, I had to resort to blunt rejection. Then, right at the end of grade nine, in the funny way these things can happen, I suddenly got a crush on him. It was the first time I had even dated seriously, and my world changed overnight. I thought Rob was the most wonderful guy I had ever met. He was an aspiring rock star and I spent every free moment I had listening while his band practiced, admiring his virtuosity on the guitar, and going to local clubs with him. He was also something of a star on the local hockey circuit and I thought this fact would impress my brothers, even though Mom was any-thing but happy about the relationship.

That summer, Tim and Tom came home for a visit and I introduced them to Rob. They were polite enough but said very little at the time. It wasn't until several weeks later when Tim phoned us one evening that I found out what they really thought about him. "By the way," Tim said just before he hung up, "are you still going out with that greaseball?"

❄

The Coupe des Alpes was my first experience of travel-ing as a member of a team, wearing a uniform, and being an official representative of Canada. I felt very proud as we gathered at the airport, waiting to board our Air Canada jet. Bob saw me off, plying me with books and magazines and obviously wishing he could come too. "You are in a wonderful position this time, Elizabeth," he said. "First time out, nothing to lose. You can just let yourself go and have fun with it."

I surprised everyone in St. Gervais, especially the team leader from the Canadian Figure Skating Association. I skated well in compulsory figures to finish fourth and followed up with two strong free-skating performances to finish a close second to Vikki de Vries of the United States. I couldn't believe it. Brian Orser won the men's event, and I watched him skate his long program, admiring his powerful jumps and fluid lines.

Mom had given me a camera to take with me, and I went around the quaint French town, snapping everything in sight and taking endless photographs of our group. After a while it got to be a joke — "Look out! Elizabeth's got her camera again!" Everyone would duck when they saw me coming. I drank it all in — the little winding streets, the pretty houses, the fascinating stores with their latticed windows. I loved every single minute of it.

In Oberstdorf, Dad came to see me skate, and that made it even more exciting for me. I wanted him, more than anyone else, to see how much I had improved and how far I had come in the skating world. Up until this point, he'd really had very little concept of what I was doing and why Mom and I were continuing to struggle so hard toward this end.

My figures weren't as good in this event as they had

been in St. Gervais, but I made up for that in the free-skating segments. I ended up winning the bronze medal, but I got a terrific ovation for the long program and actually won the free-skating phase. Barbara Graham told me that I had performed beyond the association's expectations and that they were all very pleased with me. The most important praise of all, though, came from Dad. "Elizabeth," he said, as we drove back to the hotel, "I was so proud of you I could have burst." It was what I had been waiting to hear, and I went home happy and satisfied.

Back in Canada I began to train in earnest for the 1981 competitions. It would be my first year as a Senior, and I was determined to do well. I had so many things spurring me on — my own personal drive, which was already in high gear; my intense desire to justify the faith that Mom, Bob, and Anne had shown in me; and the need to prove myself, not only to Dad, but also to the Canadian Figure Skating Association. It had occurred to me that if I could make a good impression my first time out in senior competition, someone might come forward with an offer of financial sponsorship.

Now that I had entered the world of international events, money was tighter than ever. I needed more training, more costumes, more traveling expenses. Mom and I were like two people cast adrift in a rudderless boat, being swept along in turbulent water without the power to control it. The top skaters had sponsors, agents, and major grants from the national associations, but I was a long way away from qualifying for any of those things. The only help we got was our monthly stipend from the Canadian Figure Skating Association to cover some of my skating expenses.

I spent a great deal of time with Rob still, but he was beginning to be unhappy about the pressures my training placed on me. Much of the time our social life would consist of a soft drink snatched between sessions at the rink, and it was only on Sundays that I had the time and the energy to go out with his friends and take part in all the activities they planned. On weekdays I was much too tired to do anything but drag myself back home and drop into a chair in front of the television.

❄

The Divisionals were in Nepean, and I skated just well enough to qualify for a place in the 1981 National Championships in Halifax. I was satisfied. It was my first time competing as a Senior and although I knew that it would be very unlikely for me to finish in the medals, I was ready to give it my very best shot. Bob made a deal with me right after the Divisionals: he promised that if I won a medal in Halifax, he would take me to San Diego to see the U.S. Nationals that were being held the following week. I wanted desperately to go and see all the top American skaters, so I worked feverishly and spent time with Terry Orlick, a sports psychologist who taught me relaxation techniques to help me overcome some of the tension I was feeling.

I stepped up my training schedule. I began to feel like a zombie as I plowed through session after session, trying not to think about how tired I was. I seemed to be the first person at the rink in the mornings and the last to leave at night.

Free skating was no longer the carefree, liberating experience it had once been. Bob would put me through exhausting workouts, doing axels, spins, toe loops, and salchows over and over again until I was dizzy. They had to be so secure that I could do them even when I was nervous, and that meant endless repetition. The only way to enter a jump is with complete confidence. Hesitation is fatal. "If you hesitate, even the slightest bit, you'll fall," Bob used to say.

Some days I couldn't quite get the "feel" of the ice and I would fall constantly. My body felt like a mass of bruises after one of these workouts. But no matter how I felt, I had to get up and do it over again. And again.

I left for Halifax with a fever and a sore throat. As soon as we got there, Bob took me to the competition doctors, who examined me and told me it was nothing to worry about. But I got steadily worse and had a problem getting through my numbers in practice. Finally, convinced that something was seriously wrong, Bob brought me back to the doctors. "Elizabeth is sick," he told them. "There has to be something you can do about it."

They examined me again, but could find nothing beyond the sore throat. "She just has a mild case of tonsillitis," they said. "It's making her feel bad, but it's not serious." They refused to prescribe any medication for me because of the drug-testing restrictions at the competitions. Even a small amount of medication found in a medalist's bloodstream might be cause for disqualification, and we didn't want to take any chances.

As the week wore on I grew sicker. I tried hard to pretend I wasn't, because my heart was set on getting a medal and going with Bob to San Diego, but I felt sluggish and thick-headed. I somehow made it through the compulsory figures, finishing in eighth place, and then dragged myself back to my room and fell into bed, where I stayed until the next morning. I got up to practice for the short program with every muscle in my body screaming in protest, and struggled to get through the required elements. When I came off the ice at the end of the practice I told Bob I didn't think I could compete that afternoon.

In the end I made a huge effort and managed to get through the short program. I finished in fifth place, and to everyone's astonishment I was within sight of a medal, with the long program — worth 50 percent of the total score — still to come.

I slept fitfully that night, tossing and turning and waking up frequently to find myself tense with pain. But when Bob came to pick me up for practice, I was determined not to let him know how awful I felt, so he wouldn't withdraw me from the competition. I got through the practice session and went straight back to bed until it was time to go to the arena in the evening.

As I skated on warm-up, I felt my legs trembling uncontrollably. I avoided most of the technical elements and just stroked around, fighting to get control of my body. Bob put his arm around me anxiously as I waited for my turn to skate. "It's not too late to withdraw," he said, but I wouldn't hear of it. I had come too far to think of dropping out now.

My name was announced and I skated to center ice,

trying to summon up the strength to get through the demanding program. The music started and I went into automatic performance mode, executing spins and jumps, pushing myself to follow through and keep moving. My legs were so weak and wobbly that several times they almost buckled under me. My head swam. I couldn't focus properly, and I had difficulty hearing the music. I had no idea what I was doing any more, but my body was so well drilled that it took over and I finished the routine without mishap. As I came to a stop and heard the roar of the crowd, my legs finally gave way beneath me and I collapsed in a heap on the ice. I struggled to get up, knowing that if I didn't manage to get off the ice under my own steam, I would be disqualified. The arena went silent, the audience held its breath, waiting to see what would happen. Slowly I got to my feet and stood there, swaying precariously for a moment. Then I skated to the competitors' exit where I collapsed again in Bob's arms. The crowd started to roar again, and when it was announced that I had won the bronze medal, everyone stood up.

It was a miracle that I had held on to third place, considering how sick I was. I was thrilled, but so weak I had to go straight back to bed in the hotel. Bob was concerned about my traveling to San Diego, but I was not to be put off. "A deal is a deal," I told him. I had won the medal, and I had earned the reward, sickness or no sickness. "I'll be fine by tomorrow," I assured him. "I just need some rest."

The Nationals had been exciting for many reasons, not the least of which was the fact that the Ladies event had been won by twelve-year-old Tracey Wainman, who had beaten the far more experienced Kay Thomson into second place. Fourth place had gone to Charlene Wong. The four of us began a very close relationship that February. We called ourselves "The Rat Pack," and we were the new order, the previous top skaters having retired after the 1980 Winter Olympics the year before. The other three brought flowers and gifts to my hotel room after the long program and told me how well I had done. I had just missed a place on the World Team that year, because only the first two from each event got to go to the Worlds, but with the way I was feeling it seemed like a blessing in disguise.

Bob made me return to Ottawa before we went to San Diego, so that I could have blood tests done by my family doctor. I insisted that I was well enough to go, even though I was feeling terrible and we left for California the next day.

It was a mistake from the beginning. I was unable to concentrate as I watched the competitive events. On Wednesday my doctor telephoned to say that he had the results of my tests. I had a severe case of mononucleosis.

Bob was stunned. "How on earth could those competition doctors have missed something like that?" he fumed. "They didn't even bring up the possibility." My doctor said I could stay in California for the rest of the week, but only on condition that I get plenty of rest. I felt ghastly, but I insisted on seeing every event before I left. As we sat on the plane back to Ottawa, Bob chuckled to himself. "I don't know about you, Elizabeth," he said, shaking his head in amazement. "First time out in senior Nationals and you take a bronze medal while you've got mono. I'd love to see what you can do when you're feeling okay!"

I had no scheduled events to skate during the next few weeks, and I followed my doctor's instructions rigorously, heeding his warning that rest was essential if I was to recover fully. I ate carefully, drank lots of juices, devoured tub after tub of yoghurt, and slept as much as I could. I was determined to be the healthiest skater on the circuit by the time the next season began.

Bob and Anne had made a deal with the Gloucester Skating Club which included free ice time for me, so we transferred back there in early June. Mom was pleased, because it meant a saving of about $2,500 a year. The club members were very supportive and the facilities were excellent. During the summer I passed my driving test, so I was able to get myself to and from the rink, which saved Mom hours of driving every week.

In August, Bob took me to a skating seminar in London, Ontario. During the time I was there, I attempted a triple axel, a three-and-a-half revolution jump, rarely performed by women. I prepared carefully, but when I attempted the jump, I fell. When I tried to get up, I found I couldn't stand on my right leg. It began to swell badly, so I was taken to the hospital, where the doctors put me on crutches. I had a serious sprain that kept me off the ice for three weeks. It was a long time before I tried another triple axel.

In October 1981, Barbara Graham asked me to represent the Canadian Figure Skating Association in Skate Canada. This is one of a series of international competitions held in various countries at which senior skaters compete. These competitions give skaters practice in a competitive situation, and they are held early in the season, before the national and international championships. This one was to be held in Ottawa, which was good for two reasons — I didn't have to lose any time at school, where I was in the middle of exams, and there would be no travel or hotel costs. The press took a lot of interest in the fact that a local girl was competing, and I was asked to appear on a television news show. I was getting a very small taste of things to come.

The American national champion, Rosalyn Sumners, was expected to win the gold medal in the Ladies event. She was one of the strongest of the international skaters remaining after the last Olympics, and I was very excited to be able to compete against her. I had watched her win the United States Nationals in San Diego, so I knew what a powerful competitor she was.

At the compulsory figures competition at Skate Canada, I finished way down the list, which effectively destroyed any chance I had of winning a medal, but I was still psyched up for the free-skating segments. I felt full of confidence in the short program. Everything came together for me and I landed all my jumps. As soon as I stopped, I heard the crowd roar and saw that they were all applauding wildly. It was so thrilling that I could hardly keep the tears back as I bowed and made my way to the exit. When the marks came up, I had won the short program, beating even Rosalyn. Bob hugged me. "I can't believe it!" he said. "No matter where you finish, it's this performance today that counts." In the end, I placed sixth overall, having won the short program and finished second in the long program.

Chapter Five

The Canadian Figure Skating Association made a surprise decision right after Skate Canada. They wanted me to represent Canada in the Junior World Championships in Oberstdorf in December 1981. I was still sixteen, the upper age limit for competitors at the Junior level, so I was eligible. I wondered why they weren't sending Tracey, who was younger than me. Bob thought it was to give me the experience I lacked before the next senior Worlds.

I had to adjust my long program to meet the standards of the Junior championship, taking a minute out of my existing four-minute routine. Anne worked hard on it, eliminating the medium-fast section and squeezing all the technical elements into the remainder. It was a jam-packed three minutes.

In figures, I had to roll back the clock four years. We were required to execute a forward change loop, a counter, and a back change three, none of which I had been practicing recently, but after a few days the technique came back to me. I felt I had a really good chance at a medal.

Long before I left for Oberstdorf, Barbara Graham told me that she expected me to win. She pointed out that I was the oldest skater in the event and that I was also considered to be one of the best. It was the first time that I had gone into a competition as one of the favorites, and the pressure became unnerving. I told Bob I was afraid I would let everybody down.

"Elizabeth," he said, "you are going to Germany to represent yourself, not me, not Anne, not the association, not your Mom. Just go over there and do the very best you can."

Dad had just become engaged to a woman named Betty Brousse, who worked at the same air base as he did. I was to stay with him during the competition, and he brought Betty to the airport to pick me up. I liked her immediately. I had been nervous about meeting my future stepmother and wasn't sure how I would feel about her, but she was warm and friendly and we got on very well.

The next morning we got up early to drive to the compulsory figures competition. I had drawn to skate in sixth position, and we left ourselves plenty of time to get there. Halfway to the arena, we turned a corner and encountered an enormous herd of cows, meandering slowly along the road, stopping to inspect every tuft of grass. Dad blew his horn, but that only served to make them stop completely and look round to see who was being so rude. Nothing could make them hurry, so we were forced to crawl along behind them until they reached their milking shed. By the time we reached the arena, I had only a couple of minutes to change. I had no time at all to prepare.

That may have been why I felt unsettled when I skated my first compulsory figure. I just couldn't seem to focus. The second and third figures were no better. I held on to my jumps in the short program, but fell on one of the spins. It was definitely not a very impressive performance, and going into the long program I was in seventh place.

I knew it was very unlikely that I could make up the ground I had lost in the long program, but I intended to try anyway. I was nervous in the warm-up and my legs shook, but once I began to skate my program I forgot everything else. I gave it everything I had and ended up winning the bronze medal behind Janina Wirth of East Germany and Cornelia Tesch of West Germany.

In sixth place was a young Japanese skater named Midori Ito, who came out of nowhere to skate a dazzling technical performance. She had been in eleventh place after the compulsory figures, so she was unable to win a medal, but I shall never forget her display that night. Midori was making her entrance into the international skating scene, and everyone was amazed at her talent.

Barbara Graham told me afterwards that I would have to learn to be consistent before I could really become a serious contender in senior competition. "You have to be able to do everything right on three consecutive days — three correct figures, a solid short program, and a good long program. It's not enough to have a high on one day and a low on the other." Then she smiled. "But you've definitely improved, Elizabeth — your spins are *much* better."

Clearly the officials of the Canadian Figure Skating Association were disappointed with my showing in Oberstdorf. I was upset about this, because I thought I had done my best. I went back to Ottawa with a chip on my shoulder. Bob took me to one side and gave me a lecture. He told me that if I expected to make it in the skating world, I must be prepared to accept criticism. "It's important," he said. "It's how you learn. You mustn't resent it or you'll never grow."

I went straight to the Nationals in 1982. I had placed third the previous year, so I was allowed to skip the Sectionals and Divisionals. This year the competition was to be held in Brandon, Manitoba, and I knew my main rivals would be the three other members of the Rat Pack — Charlene, Kay, and Tracey. I wondered which order we would finish in this year.

From the outset of the competition it was obvious to everyone that Tracey was in trouble. She had been suffering from a severe bout of stomach flu and had difficulty with every segment of the event.

I was fifth after compulsory figures, but I won the short program and pulled up to third place. I felt I now had a good chance to take the bronze medal if I could only hold my own during the free skating. I felt confident as I waited to hear my name announced, and from the moment my music started I just seemed to fly across the ice. I skated a clean long program, playing to the audience and enjoying their reaction. I finished second and took the silver medal, right behind Kay Thomson. Tracey took the bronze medal. Bob and Anne hugged me in delight. "Well done, Elizabeth," Anne said. "I'm so proud of you."

There was a sad edge to my personal triumph, however. Tracey had taken her defeat very hard. She was devastated by her performance, not really able to grasp what had happened to her. She had been Canada's sweetheart when she won the gold medal the year before and had become a national media celebrity and a household name, but all the attention had taken its toll and she had been unable to maintain her number-one status. Kay, Charlene, and I tried to cheer her up, but she obviously felt terrible. It was difficult for the rest of us to celebrate, knowing how hard she had taken it.

❄

It wasn't until I got back to Ottawa that I really began to think about the World Championships. I was thrilled at the prospect of going to Copenhagen and competing against all the other top skaters. I told Mom we would be able to go sightseeing when the events were over. She looked at me sadly. "I wish that could happen," she said. "But it just isn't possible. We simply don't have the money for me to come too. I'll have to wait until next time." I knew she was right, but I was very disappointed.

A couple of weeks before I was due to leave for Denmark, the Gloucester club held a send-off celebration for me. I was one of the few skaters from the Ottawa area who were competing at the world level, so they wanted to wish me luck. There was a pleasant reception, and just before it was over, the president of the club handed

Mom an envelope. "This is from all of us," she said. "We wanted you to be able to share this experience with Elizabeth." Inside the envelope were all the expenses for Mom to go to Denmark with me. Mom's eyes filled with tears — she couldn't believe the club had arranged something like that for her. It was one of the kindest things anyone has ever done for us.

Copenhagen was very exciting for me. It is a magical city, home of Hans Christian Andersen and the marvelous Tivoli Gardens, and we arrived to find the streets bathed in bright spring sunshine and the trees bursting into new bud. Everyone in the skating world seemed to be there, from East and West, famous faces from past competitions and all the top names of the present. On top of all that, I discovered that Dad had managed to arrange some leave so he could drive to Copenhagen to join us. I was so happy — I would have both parents there to watch me compete.

Bob picked me up from the hotel next morning and drove me to the arena for the compulsories. He talked to me all the way over, calming me down, and making me focus on what lay ahead. I warmed up in the early-morning chill of the rink, trying to stop my legs from trembling, waiting for my turn to skate. I wanted so much to do well.

Unfortunately I lost my concentration while I was laying out my first figure and I missed the center completely. I couldn't believe what I had done, and I knew I would be heavily penalized. The judges at the World Championships tend to deal severely with the lesser-known skaters and to be much more lenient with the top contenders. Sure enough, they came down on me like a ton of bricks, and I was in thirty-third position out of thirty-five after the first figure. I was devastated. I ran to the dressing room and burst into tears. Mom came in and tried to comfort me, but I cried uncontrollably. I knew I had destroyed any hopes I had of finishing in the top ten.

After a while, I dried my tears and pulled myself together. I had only myself to blame, and I still had a long way to go before the competition was over. I did much better in the second and third figures, and pulled up fourteen places to finish nineteenth after the combined figures. It was an improvement on thirty-third, but I was still upset with myself. I could have done so much better.

Mom and Dad took me out for dinner, trying their best to console me. Dad was in one of his funny moods, telling jokes and making us laugh. It was impossible to be depressed around him, and I began to relax and enjoy myself. As he was saying goodnight to me, Dad told me he had made an appointment for me to get my hair done in the hotel salon the following morning. He knew that it would improve my spirits.

Right after practice the next morning, I made for the beauty salon and had my hair washed and set by a charming Danish stylist who communicated with me in pidgin English. As I was sitting in a chair that faced on to the street, I saw Dad passing outside. He saw me and stopped, waving his hand toward a huge bag he was carrying. Then he pulled out an Arctic-type sweater coat and made signs to indicate that he had bought it for me, and did I like it? I grinned because it was gorgeous, thick cream-colored wool with a gray pattern woven into it. Dad draped it around his shoulders, modeling it for me. Then he reached down into the bag and pulled out a matching scarf, which he promptly wound around his head, and a pair of gloves. There he was, prancing around in the street, wearing all this stuff and making silly faces at me though the hotel window. Half the people in the salon thought he looked ridiculous, and the people walking past him in the street gave him a wide berth. Dad had bought the outfit to cheer me up, and I shall always love him for that gesture. I still have it today.

I was in an utterly different frame of mind when I went in to skate the short program that afternoon. I had lost my apprehension, and I was intent on skating the very best I knew how. I skated strongly, moving up two places to finish seventeenth. In the long program, I stumbled early on and almost lost my balance on a triple toe jump, but I recovered and managed to pull up four more places. I was thirteenth in the final standings. The new champion was Elaine Zayak of the United States. Bob was pleased, especially since I had placed eighth overall in the combined free skating. He told me it was a very promising beginning for my first time at the World Championships.

When I struggled off the plane at Ottawa airport, toting a mass of hand luggage, I was startled to be greeted by a large group of cheering friends and fellow skaters. Flowers and packages were thrust at me, and everyone wanted to hug and kiss me. It was a bit overwhelming. Even Betty Stewart, the mayor of Gloucester, was there.

I was exhausted, but I did a television interview

before I left the airport. "What did you think when you saw the crowd?" asked the interviewer.

I laughed. "I thought there must have been someone famous on the plane."

"How about that first figure?"

"A disaster," I answered. "It was so stupid of me — the team leader told me I looked like I was skating in a cloud."

"But you moved up with each phase of the competition?"

"Yes. But it was tough. A bit like trying to eat peanut butter through a straw."

❄

I came home to a busy round of exhibitions and a heavy schedule of schoolwork to make up for lost time. Rob and I began to fight because I couldn't spend much time with him. Eventually he broke off our relationship, telling me he just couldn't put up with this any longer. He wanted to go out with someone who would be free to spend time with him, joining his friends in the activities they were always planning. He complained that I was never available, and that even when I was, I was too tired to go anywhere. I was terribly upset. I knew he was right, but Rob had been my first boyfriend and I thought that the world had come to an end when we split. I cried and cried about it.

As the spring wore on, however, I met someone new. Mark Grady was the Zamboni driver at the arena, quieter than Rob and more accepting of my career. We started to date, and before long we were a steady item. Rob Forcier was forgotten.

On April 16, I was chosen as one of 282 "young achievers" to attend a dinner for Her Majesty, Queen Elizabeth, Prince Philip, and Prime Minister Pierre Elliott Trudeau. My name was put forward by Lloyd Francis, the Liberal MP for my riding. I was very excited — I was going to meet the Queen. I worried about how to curtsy properly and what to say.

The dinner was wonderful. I was seated at table 3, right in front of the Queen's table. I had a clear view and was fascinated by her — she was more beautiful than she looks in photographs, with a flawless skin and very clear blue eyes. After dinner, Prime Minister Trudeau accompanied the Queen as she moved through the guests. When they got to me, he introduced me to her, and she gave me one of her rare dazzling smiles. It was an evening I shall remember forever.

❋

Bob, Anne, and I had a conference about the future. My small size and weight were both an advantage and a disadvantage at this point in my life. At four foot ten inches, I weighed ninety-five pounds. My center of balance was lower than it is with most skaters, giving me a competitive advantage in landing the more difficult jumps. On the other hand, my compulsory figure tracings were always very faint and hard to see on the ice. I had to work extra hard to follow their outlines. We discussed how to compensate for this, talked about programs, and plotted ways to improve my consistency.

Finances were still a struggle for us, but because I was competing internationally, I was finally eligible for funding from both the government and the association. I had a B-card from Sport Canada, which meant I was ranked in the top sixteen in my sport internationally, and entitled me to $6600 a year toward expenses. I had also begun to receive funding from the Athletes' Trust of the Canadian Figure Skating Association, $4900 for the year 1982-83. Barbara Graham told me that the association was satisfied with my performance in Copenhagen. It was then that I knew I must have broken through some invisible barrier. For the first time, I began to entertain thoughts about the possibility of becoming a champion and about representing Canada in the Olympic Games.

Chapter Six

Somewhere along the line, in the late summer of 1982, my life began to spin out of control. Nobody seemed to notice, least of all me, but later I could look back and see all the warning signs.

I had just turned seventeen and was caught up in all the glamor and excitement of the international skating scene. It was heady stuff for me, being around all the big names, going to all the parties and receptions that surrounded international skating events. I was the new kid on the circuit, and I loved the celebrity and all the perks. I had spent years with my nose pressed against the windows of the candy store and now I was finally inside I intended to savor every single minute of it.

I spent the summer in Toronto, working at the Cricket Club with the noted Dutch coach, Ellen Burka. She was widely considered to be the preeminent artistic coach in the country, and she taught skaters an overall approach to performing, giving equal emphasis to music appreciation, dance training, choreography, and dramatic interpretation. She was also a stickler for flawless technique, including stroking classes in each day's training. She emphasized the importance of stroking in improving cardiovascular performance, posture, and balance, and made us concentrate on body position and maneuvering on the edge of the blade. Her most famous student, Toller Cranston, had been largely responsible for revolutionizing men's skating, introducing opera to the ice and incorporating daringly innovative movements into his competitive routines.

The weeks passed quickly and I lost fourteen pounds under Mrs. Burka's scrutiny. I also took part in her Theater on Ice sessions, where she taught us to act out dramatic scenes in conjunction with the choreography. I enjoyed these evenings, and learned to view the ice as a stage rather than as a sporting forum.

At the end of the summer, I returned to Ottawa in time to be at Dad's wedding — he and Betty had formed a close and loving bond, and I was glad that Dad had found such happiness. It was a quiet ceremony, just family and a few close friends, in a small church in Ottawa.

In early October I was chosen to represent Canada in Skate America. It was my first major competition since Copenhagen, and for the first time in my career I would be coming into an event as one of the top medal contenders.

A week before we were set to leave, I woke up at five in the morning and couldn't open my eyes properly. They felt tight and strange. I got out of bed cautiously — every muscle in my body was sore and stiff. I went to look in the bathroom mirror, and what I saw made me gasp aloud. My whole face was swollen, and my eyes peered from two narrow slits.

I called Mom. "Oh, my God," she said when she saw me. "What on earth happened to you?" She made me get dressed and we drove straight to the emergency room at the hospital.

I stayed there for hours, undergoing all kinds of tests and answering questions. Mom called Bob, and he arrived half an hour later. "Oh my poor Elizabeth," he said, hugging me.

The doctors gave us an ointment which cleared up the problem in a few days, but I couldn't practice during that time because I still couldn't see properly. That left me with two days to rehearse before I left. I considered withdrawing, but as my face improved, my confidence returned.

By the time Bob and I boarded the plane for Lake Placid, I felt fine. We drove to the hotel and everyone I knew seemed to be there. I was so excited, I rushed around, giving out my room number and making plans. I was invited to three parties the first night, and I went to all of them, catching up on gossip and exchanging stories until well after midnight. When I finally got to bed I was far too excited to sleep.

The competition began the next morning. My compulsory figures were a disaster. I missed the center of my loop not once but twice and knew I was in trouble. Bob stood watching by the boards, shaking his head in disbelief. When the totals were in, I was in fourteenth place and I was furious with myself.

The afternoon practice session went well, however, and by the time Mom and I sat down to an early dinner in the hotel restaurant I was feeling relatively confident again. I was facing an almost impossible task, but free skating was my strongest suit and I was determined to pull it off, in spite of the practice time I'd lost. I ordered carefully, choosing a small steak, mushrooms, wild rice, and cauliflower. The dessert tray was filled with tempting cakes and pastries, but I managed to resist them and ordered a cup of tea instead.

Back in my room I watched television for a while, but I found myself wondering what everyone else was doing. I called two of my friends and asked if they would like to come up to my room. I figured I wouldn't be able to sleep anyway, so I might as well have some company until I got tired. The three of us talked about what we had done during the summer, sipping on diet Coke and nibbling on peanuts.

I had drawn last for the short program next afternoon. I felt oddly detached and disoriented, not really up for it, and I missed one of the vital compulsory elements. Even so, I finished fairly strongly and managed to pull up to ninth position. With the long program still to come, I felt I still had a fighting chance. It wasn't over yet.

Bob called out to me as I was leaving the building. "Walk back to the hotel with me, Elizabeth," he said. "I need to talk to you." He sounded subdued, not at all like his usual cheery self, and we walked in silence for a while.

Finally he said, "Elizabeth, I'm worried about you. You're losing your concentration. You used to attack everything, but now you seem to be holding back." He paused and looked at me seriously. "You can't have it both ways. If you want to be a champion, you have to give up everything else. You can't compromise. I know you've been sick, but you just have to get past that and give it one hundred percent."

I knew he was right, of course, but I wasn't sure I could do it. I wasn't sure I was up for that kind of commitment. "I'll try," I promised him. "I'll do the very best I can."

As we parted, he put a hand on my arm. "Please, Elizabeth," he pleaded, "go to bed early. Get some rest." I told him not to worry.

That night I found it very difficult to sleep. I could hear the sounds of partying coming from some of the other rooms and the noise was hard to shut out. The music from my long program — Tchaikovsky's *Romeo and Juliet* — kept running through my head over and over again, and I tossed and turned restlessly.

When I arrived at the arena the next evening, the stands were filled. The long program always attracted the largest crowds, and I could feel the excitement in the air. I was skating in the final group, and I paced around backstage, trying to block everything out of my mind. I was faintly aware of the applause coming from the arena and the chatter of the other girls gathered around the dressing rooms, but I fought to keep my concentration. At last it was our turn to warm up. I was in great form, and as soon as I got on the ice I felt the tension leave me.

When my name was announced, I skated to center ice and drew a deep breath, focusing hard, waiting for the first bars of my music to fill the air. When it started, I flew across the ice, the audience invisible to me, the judges forgotten. I landed a good double axel, then a solid double loop. Everything was flowing easily and I began to feel secure. Suddenly I became aware of the audience clapping, and for a split second I stopped thinking about my choreography. As I took off for the first part of the combination jump, I slipped and fell. I was up in an instant, but lost my edge and fell again. I was devastated. I couldn't understand what was happening. I managed to recover enough to finish the rest of the program cleanly, but when I came off the ice I hardly dared even look at Bob. I knew how disappointed he would be. When the marks came up I saw they were actually better than I expected. I had finished in eighth position overall and had placed third in the free-skating segment. I turned to Bob, relieved, but he didn't say anything. He was clearly upset.

I couldn't bear to face Mom that night. I felt guilty, thinking I had let her down. She had worked so hard to pay for all my training and had put such faith in me. I shut myself in my room and sat on my bed with my arms clasped around my knees, staring into space. I wasn't sure how much longer I could go on letting Mom make these sacrifices for my skating career. I wasn't even sure I wanted to continue.

Back in Ottawa, Barbara Graham talked to Mom about my poor showing in Skate America. The two of them discussed my strengths and weaknesses, and came to the conclusion that it might be a good idea for me to change coaches. Bob McAvoy had brought me a long way, Barbara said, but he was still quite young and a more experienced coach would sharpen my technique and give me the extra polish I needed if I were going to continue to compete internationally.

Mom knew there was a certain logic to this thinking, but she dreaded having to tell Bob. He had been there for me through the bad times and the good times, refusing to take any fees when he knew money was tight. "You can give it to me later," he would tell Mom. "I'll only spend it, anyway, if you pay me now." For eight years he had encouraged me, cheered me on, offered friendship and advice, and let me cry on his shoulder. Most of all, he had believed in me when it really counted. It seemed so cruel to be leaving him now, when all his hard work seemed about to pay off.

Eventually, it was settled that I should go to Emmerich Danzer in Lake Placid, the acknowledged expert where teaching the discipline of figures is concerned. I was to go down for the start of the new season and train with him throughout the winter. What happened after that would depend on my performance in the competitions.

No one asked my opinion. In fact, I knew nothing about it until Mom sat me down one evening and told me I would be going to live in Lake Placid, and would be working with a new coach. I was still very immature and naive at that age, and I accepted what my mother told me without question. I knew I would miss Bob, of course, but I was excited at the prospect of going to live in Lake Placid.

In theory, the plan was a good one. My figures needed to improve and Emmerich, who had been world champion from 1966 to 1968, was one of the best figure coaches in the world. But in retrospect, I can see that the move was premature. The timing was wrong and I wasn't emotionally mature enough to handle two major changes at once. I not only had to leave home, but also the Gloucester club and Bob McAvoy. My emotional ties to home, school, and familiar club were cut and I was thrown into an alien environment which I found unsettling. And so I passed from one set of problems to another, and for quite different reasons I found myself unable to cope with them. None of this was the fault of my coaches — Bob and Emmerich were top-notch professionals — but we didn't understand that at the time.

When the car was all packed up, Mom drove me to Bob's house to say goodbye. When he opened the door he glanced at me briefly and then looked away again without a word.

I felt a lump rising in my throat. "Bob, aren't you going to wish me luck?"

When he turned his head to look at me I could see anger in his face. "You think a new coach is going to solve all your problems," he said. "You're wrong. It's you that's the problem, Elizabeth. If you don't change your attitude, you'll never be a champion."

I gasped and turned away, walking quickly back to the car before he could see the tears running down my cheeks. His words had shocked me deeply. I had sought his approval for so long, relied on his judgement for so many years, that this rejection was unbearable. It shook my belief in myself.

As we drove out of Gloucester, I tried to come to grips with Bob's words. "I don't understand, Mom," I said miserably. "He was always the one who believed in me.

He used to tell me I could go all the way to the top. Now it seems like he hates me."

Mom reached over and squeezed my hand. "He doesn't hate you," she said. "Believe me, when you make the world team, no one will be prouder than Bob."

I wanted to believe her, but I couldn't come to terms with the feeling of loss and rejection.

❊

Mom had discovered a great house in Lake Placid for me to stay in. It belonged to a lady named Patty Stewart, and she lived there with her mother. The two of them worked as cooks at a private boarding school in Northwood, an exclusive residential area. They welcomed us warmly when we arrived, helping us to carry all my boxes upstairs. I had a lovely room, with a desk and bookshelves and even a small television set. A large window with white curtains overlooked the back garden. I set out my books and photographs and put my beloved old teddy bear on the bed. It was beginning to look a little bit more like home.

In the afternoon, Mom and I went for a walk. Lake Placid is a fairy-tale town, set amidst dark evergreens and pines and curled around the shores of a blue, sparkling lake. The air smelled fresh and sweet, with a faint hint of wood smoke, and we wandered down the main street, looking into shop windows and munching on some delicious local fudge. I had remembered Lake Placid as a busy, bustling place, filled with vacationers and competitors attending the skating championships I had entered there, but now it was quiet and deserted.

Very few people were about, and in the late October twilight it seemed almost to be asleep.

Back at the house, Patty and her mother invited us to join them for an early dinner. We ate in the big cheerful kitchen, tucking into large helpings of Patty's marvelous chicken pot pie, followed by generous slices of apple strudel with whipped cream. She was an excellent cook, and insisted that we have seconds of everything. I could hardly move as I rose to help clear the table, and I was glad I didn't have to skate until the next day.

I went up to bed early, leaving Mom reading by the fire. After I had turned out the light, I stood for a moment at the window, looking down into the moonlit garden. I still hadn't fully accepted that Bob was no longer my coach, but I was looking forward to meeting Emmerich and his wife, Margie, who worked with him. I had no inkling of what this peaceful place had in store for me, not yet realizing how much my life was about to change.

Chapter Seven

The next morning, Mom drove me to the arena and we met Emmerich and Margie. I liked them both immediately, and as soon as Mom left for her long drive back to Ottawa, I laced up my skates and began to show them all my elements. Emmerich complimented me on some things and criticized others. He felt we had a great deal of ground to cover if I was to be ready for the Canadian National Championships in February. I was a willing student, eager to please him, wanting to win his approval. At the end of the morning he told me I could stop and asked me not to be late the next morning. I went home, exhausted from the workout, aching in every muscle. It had been more than a week since I'd skated and I was already out of shape.

At the end of the first week, Emmerich told me that I could be very successful if I kept working hard and concentrated on my compulsory figures. He made arrangements for me to skate an extra patch three evenings a week. "It's not going to be easy, Elizabeth," he told me. "You've got a lot of work ahead of you. But I feel you can do it."

For some reason, I found myself wondering if I could. I wasn't happy. I still missed Bob terribly, and I was very homesick. I called Mom, pouring out my miseries to her on the phone. She was sympathetic, but assured me that I would soon start to feel better. "Give it time, Elizabeth," she said. "I know how you feel, but I promise you it'll get better. It'll be the weekend before you know it, and I'll be down again."

True to her promise, Mom came down every weekend, and I began to live for Saturday mornings when she would arrive, laden with goodies from home, bringing me favorite books and news from my friends. For a while, her visits made the rest of the week bearable, but as time went on the gap between weekends seemed to get longer and longer. I always felt an emptiness inside me when I watched her drive away again.

Gradually I established a routine, leaving the house at five each morning and hurrying through the predawn streets to the arena. Once inside I would warm up until Emmerich and Margie arrived, and then we would work on figures, tracing endless loops, one after the other. In the mid-morning, we would have a light breakfast in a local coffee shop, and afterward I would free skate until lunch time. Most days Emmerich and Margie ate lunch with me, and I looked forward to that, always enjoying the conversations we had. The afternoons I spent in my room, sprawled across the bed, lost in the soaps and munching potato chips. I never went anywhere. I was

supposed to keep up my school work with correspondence courses, but after a while, I found myself doing
less and less studying and I eventually stopped doing
the lessons altogether.

Three times a week I would return to the arena in the
late afternoon for an extra session. Sometimes
Emmerich and Margie would bring me back to their
house for dinner afterward. I longed for those times,
feeling the awful loneliness go away in the warm circle of
their family.

Some of the local kids were friendly to me, but I made
excuses not to go out with them. Part of the problem
was that I had very little money, but I had no desire to
socialize anyway. I didn't understand it — I had always
been so gregarious, so ready for any kind of fun. Now I
had become reclusive, avoiding situations where I
would run into people I knew, spending most of my free
time shut safely inside my room. It became my sanctuary, its pale blue walls shielding me from the outside
world, cutting me off from reality.

Shortly after I arrived, Emmerich began to have some
serious problems with the arena staff. I had no idea
what was wrong, but the situation created an uncomfortable atmosphere, and Emmerich kept strictly to his
own teaching area, avoiding any contact with the staff.
As soon as our sessions were finished, he would hurry
us out of the building and drive me back to my house. I
had no opportunity to hang out with any of the other
skaters after practice and so I became even more
isolated.

Patty and her mother left the house in the late morning to prepare lunch at the school. They returned in the

afternoon for a couple of hours and then went back to make snacks. They were seldom around when I was there, and I spent most of my time in the house alone. Even when they had an evening off and invited me to join them for a game of cards, I would refuse. I had grown used to my own company and couldn't bring myself to be sociable. I just couldn't seem to make the effort.

Obviously I was becoming increasingly depressed and lonely. But I couldn't seem to break the spiral – loneliness made me reclusive, which made me even lonelier. Sometimes I would arrange to go over to some-one's house in the evening, but when the time came to leave I would always telephone and make an excuse. After a while, people stopped inviting me. The nights were hard. Sometimes I would toss and turn for hours, trying desperately to stop my mind going round in cir-cles. At other times I would oversleep and find it very difficult to get out of bed in the mornings. Often, when I did fall asleep, I would have nightmares, waking up with a start, sweating and terrified.

Mom continued to come on weekends. Things weren't so bad when she was there, and we would play cards and talk and take drives around the lake. I was careful not to let her know how unhappy I was because I knew how much it was costing her to keep me there. It was a constant struggle for her to make ends meet, and it was terribly important to her that my new training regime worked out. There was no way in the world that I was going to let her know there was anything wrong with me.

Gradually, almost imperceptibly at first, I began to gain weight. One Sunday evening as she watched me struggling to zip up my blue jeans, Mom asked anxiously, "Are you putting on weight?" I assured her that it was nothing to worry about, just a pound or two. I would soon lose it.

Later that same week, Margie took me aside after practice. She looked worried. "I think you should start watching what you eat, Elizabeth. Perhaps you should cut out the snacks." As soon as I got home, I examined myself carefully in the bathroom mirror. Margie was right. I *was* gaining weight. I could see it around my waist and hips. I threw out two bags of potato chips and a box of cookies. Then I went out and bought a large bag of apples and oranges and a pack of sugarless gum.

By the end of November I had withdrawn so far into myself that I was unable to cope with even the simplest occurrence outside my narrow daily routine. I wanted desperately to have friends, but did everything in my power to discourage them. One of the girls at the arena had a birthday and invited me to her party. I had always loved parties, and this time I was determined to go and enjoy myself. I told myself over and over again that I could make it, but as the day approached I started to panic.

When the evening finally came I washed my hair, put on a new dress, and waited for the other kids to come by and pick me up. Patty and her mother were at the school, so I was alone in the house. I sat at the bottom of the stairs and listened for the sound of the car, my hands gripping the banister. My heart began to pound and my mouth went dry, and when I heard the car stop outside I couldn't get up. A horn blasted twice, and then I heard someone run up the front steps and knock on the door. I sat very still, waiting for them to leave, not making a sound. After they drove away I sat there for a long time, tears sliding down my face, wondering if I should call a taxi, but knowing I didn't really want to.

I stopped eating lunch altogether, figuring that if I lived on two meals a day I would be certain to lose weight. I avoided anything with sugar or starch. I had my own fridge in the kitchen, and I stocked it with carrots and celery and a whole selection of fruit and nuts. In spite of my efforts, however, I continued to gain weight. My neck and face puffed up, and none of my clothes fitted properly any more. One weekend in November, Mom ran her hand over the back of my neck. "Good heavens," she said, alarmed. "There's enough flesh here for me to pick you up like a puppy."

I was making steady progress at the rink, but Emmerich was unhappy with me. "You're not fooling anyone, Elizabeth," he said severely. "Only one thing makes you gain weight and that's calories." He was convinced I was a closet binger. I cut down my intake even further, having only clear soup and fruit during the day and taking smaller helpings at dinner. I hadn't bought a candy bar or a bag of potato chips in weeks.

I was hurt by Emmerich's lack of trust, but I understood it. It made no sense that I was still gaining weight. I didn't go to a doctor for help because I was terrified of diet pills. I knew too many girls who had become dependent on them. Somehow I convinced myself that this was only a temporary situation, that my system would adjust itself if I just waited long enough.

At the same time, in the middle of all this concern about weight, I noticed something else. This time it was a welcome surprise. My skin, which had always been plagued by outbreaks of eczema, was clear and flawless for the first time in my life.

In early December, I was chosen to represent Canada officially in Skate Moscow, and I forgot all about my problems in the excitement and anticipation of seeing the Soviet Union. Mom warned me that I mustn't drink the water, so I packed lots of bottled spring water. I also took several boxes of kleenex and two large bath towels. Emmerich and I flew over on an Aeroflot jet, landing in Moscow on a clear, sunny day. The city was not the grim, forbidding place I had expected to find, but was mysterious and ancient, sparkling under a blanket of fresh snow. We were taken on a tour, marveling at the unforgettable sight of Red Square, the imposing walls of the Kremlin stretched along one side, the astonishing onion domes of St. Basil's Cathedral standing guard at the entrance. I was fascinated and told our guide that I thought it would make a wonderful setting for an outdoor ice show. He replied in polite but slightly repressive tones that nothing so frivolous could be contemplated in the shadow of Lenin's tomb.

The Russians made excellent hosts and we were entertained with lavish parties every night. My fears and depression completely vanished, and I found myself having more fun than anybody. I thoroughly enjoyed all the receptions surrounding the competitions and took part enthusiastically in whatever activities were arranged for us. I didn't skate particularly well, finishing eighth overall, but Emmerich seemed satisfied. Sitting on the plane back to New York, I was convinced that I had finally turned my life around.

I couldn't have been more wrong. Back in Lake Placid the reclusive pattern returned immediately. If anything, it seemed to be more severe than it had been before the trip to Moscow. The simple act of going out of the house now became a major undertaking, and even phone calls posed a threat to me. I always made it to practice, but had completely abandoned any idea of socializing. I no longer wanted to try.

I made an enormous effort to hide all this from the Danzers, terrified that they would refuse to work with me if they knew the full extent of my problems. I tried hard to block out all emotion, stifle any feelings, but it was difficult. Every day I felt myself slipping a little further downhill. I had always been a fighter, but now I seemed to have lost all my spirit. I felt scared all the time.

Things ceased to matter to me. I had no idea why — I didn't understand what was happening. I simply stopped caring. I reached the point at which I didn't even want to have lessons. I felt Emmerich was crowding me and I wanted only to skate on my own. I didn't want to have to speak to anyone, and I didn't have the nerve to tell him about it. I went through the motions of practicing every day and bolted back to the house the moment the sessions were over.

As Christmas approached, the town began to come to life. Colored lights surrounded shop windows and bright decorations were strung across the main street of the town. Snow fell, making the surrounding mountains white and beautiful. The inevitable round of festivities began, and I was invited to some parties. I gave the usual excuses, no longer hesitating before I turned them down. I refused to think about what I was doing.

Although originally Mom had planned to come to Lake Placid for Christmas, I was able to take off a couple of days and go home to Ottawa for the holidays, even though the Eastern Canadian Championships were coming up in January and I was far from ready for them.

I went Christmas shopping for something to give Mom. All the gift shops in Lake Placid seemed to be laden with Olympic souvenirs left over from the winter games of 1980. I wasn't sure if they had made too many at the time, or if they had just decided they were on to a good thing. At any rate, I finally found a nice set of coffee mugs with figure skaters painted on them.

Shortly before I left for Ottawa, I had a turkey dinner with Emmerich and Margie. Emmerich gave me a pin from the 1968 Olympics, and talked about his own career. Up to that point, I hadn't realized what a legend he was in the skating world, and I began to see him in a new light.

Mom and I spent Christmas quietly at home. At midnight I handed Mom her present. "They're lovely, Elizabeth," she said. Then she handed me a parcel. "For you. I hope you like it."

When I tore off the paper I found a beautiful white jacket inside. "Oh, Mom. You shouldn't have bought this for me. It must have cost so much money."

She reached forward and hugged me. "I don't want to hear another word," she said, helping me into it. She zipped it up and turned the collar up around my face. It was a perfect fit. "I want you to feel pretty when you go to the Canadians this year."

Later we opened a bottle of "bubbly" (our word for diet soda) and Mom lifted her glass to me. "To you, Elizabeth. I don't know what the year has in store for you, but whatever it is, I know you're going to make it."

Chapter Eight

The next week brought a new crisis into my life. My hair was beginning to fall out. I noticed that the drain was clogged with hair after I took a shower, and then I saw hair on my pillow when I woke in the mornings. I phoned Mom in a panic.

"Don't worry, Elizabeth," she reassured me. "It's winter. I'm sure it's just old hair coming out."

I wanted to believe her. She was always right about things. But as the days passed I grew more and more nervous about it. When I ran my hands through my hair, it came out in clumps. This was not simply old hair coming out. It had to be something far more serious.

The next week Mom came down for the weekend and took me to a local hairdresser to get a hot oil treatment. She figured that should take care of the problem. When the stylist had finished rinsing my hair, she called Mom over to the basin. "I think you should take a look," she said quietly. I heard Mom gasp and struggled to sit up.

"What is it?" I demanded.

Mom didn't say anything at first.

"Mom, *please*. Tell me what's wrong."

She looked at me for a moment, then reached over to pick up a hand mirror. She held it so I could see the back of my head. "You have to know sometime, Elizabeth. Look at the crown of your head."

I stared at my reflection and saw that all the hair had gone from the crown — I was left with a bald spot the size of a jelly-jar lid.

Back at the house, Mom tried to persuade me to come back to Ottawa. Even though I had always tried to hide it, she knew I was homesick and thought perhaps this was the real reason for my physical problems. "There's no disgrace in giving up," she said. "You've given it your best shot down here, and no one can ask for more than that."

But something in me had changed, hardened. I felt some of my old determination returning. I wasn't about to quit at this point. I had my heart set on competing in the National Championships and was intent on seeing it through.

"Mom, I can't give up yet," I said. "I have to keep trying. The hairdresser said that the hair loss might reverse itself, so I'll just keep hoping that happens. If things are no better by the spring, then I'll come home."

Mom knew my mind was made up, and she didn't argue. As she started her car to drive home, I leaned in the window and kissed her. For a moment I was tempted to give in right then and go with her, but I didn't say anything. I was determined to stick it out.

I was working hard to prepare for the Eastern Championships to be held in January 1983. They were the preliminary qualifying event prior to the February National Championships. I was skating extra sessions, concentrating hard on my technique. I was now almost twenty pounds overweight, but there was nothing I could do except ignore it. I was eating so little by then that it was beginning to affect my strength. I tired easily and had to stop frequently to catch my breath. My hair continued to come out steadily. I called Mom one evening.

"Mom, I'm still gaining weight and losing my hair," I told her. "If only I could switch them over, I'd be in great shape."

I had a small frame and every extra pound on me showed like five or six would on a taller person. I must have looked like a blimp.

I was expected to place in the top three at the Eastern Canadian championships, based on my showing at the previous year's Worlds. As it was, I barely managed to hold on to fourth place, narrowly qualifying for the National Championships. Emmerich was beside himself, convinced that my failure to win a medal had something to do with my weight and that I must be gorging in secret to have put on so many extra pounds. He told me coldly that I had less than three weeks before Nationals to pull myself together. He was at a loss to know how to help me and I know he felt as though he had failed with me.

By the end of January I could no longer hide my hair loss from the Danzers. I had been combing the back up and teasing it to cover the bare patch, but by now it was painfully obvious. Almost all my hair had gone from the back and sides and there was a bald patch at the crown. I was left with a ring of hair, rather like a monk's tonsure. The Danzers reacted with immediate sympathy, realizing that something must be terribly wrong. Emmerich knew now that I had been telling him the truth about my diet. He said he had never known anything like it in all his years of teaching.

One Monday afternoon, Margie came to see me at the house. She sat on my bed and put her arm around me. "Elizabeth," she said, "Barbara Graham called me from the Canadian Figure Skating Association. She suggested that you might want to withdraw from the Nationals."

I drew back instinctively, feeling the now-familiar sense of hurt and rejection. I stared at Margie. "What about you?" I asked. "What do you and Emmerich think?"

Margie shook her head. "It doesn't matter what we think. It's between you and the association."

"It matters to me," I replied fiercely. "It matters very much. You're the only people who have any right to say anything, you and Mom."

Margie hesitated for a moment. "Elizabeth, you are the one who has to go through this. I want you to think about it very carefully before you decide. You'll be going in with half your hair gone and twenty pounds of extra weight. It's not going to be easy. No one will blame you if you decide to drop out."

"But what about you?" I repeated stubbornly. "I want to know what you and Emmerich think."

After a pause, Margie said, "If you decide to continue, then Emmerich and I are one hundred percent behind you. We'll help you in any way we can."

I let out a breath of relief. "Then that's settled. I'll stay in. I'm not a quitter, Margie. I've come this far and there's no way I'm going to drop out now."

She hugged me tightly. "I thought you might say that. But it will be difficult for you. There are all kinds of rumors flying around."

"What kind of rumors?" I asked, shocked. "What are people saying about me?"

"They're saying you have leukemia. That you have been undergoing chemotherapy. Some people are even saying you've been doing drugs. You'll have to cope with all that talk."

As she got up to go, she turned to me again. "No matter how you finish in the Nationals, I just want you to know that the important thing is that you tried. Emmerich and I are proud of you for that."

❄

I redoubled my efforts in the few remaining days before leaving for the Canadian Championships in Montreal. I jogged twice a day down by the lake, worked out in the weight room at the arena, did push-ups, and skipped rope. Mom got in touch with the CTV network, who were covering the events, and begged them not to show me in close-up. When she explained the situation, they were sympathetic and promised to do their best.

In Montreal I was greeted with incredulous stares from some of the other competitors, but I tried not to let it get to me. Charlene Wong was there, and I was so pleased to see her again that I almost forgot about my appearance. I was relieved to see Tracey Wainman, who had been going through some severe emotional problems of her own at the time. The two of us spent a lot of time together, sharing confidences and trying to bolster each other's ego.

"Remember how the guys all used to make bets about which one of them would go bald first?" I joked. "Well, wait till I tell them who hit the jackpot! Gordon Forbes will be relieved to know he wasn't the first after all."

The competition got off to a good start and I skated the best figures of my career so far. Emmerich was encouraging, saying that if I did really well in the freestyle I could win a medal, and I was determined to give it everything I had. I still hadn't encountered the public's reaction to my appearance, since no one turned out to watch figures other than the coaches and the other competitors, but I tried not to think about it.

Mom took me to a small French restaurant for dinner and encouraged me to relax. Just before we got up to leave, she reached across the table and took my hand. "It's not too late to drop out," she said. "You don't have to do this, you know." I could see that she was almost in tears.

"Oh, yes I do, Mom. I have to do it. I have to see it through," I replied. "And now that I've done well in the figures, I'd be nuts to stop."

The following afternoon was the short program, and I began to feel apprehensive as I waited for my warm-up group to be called. As I was leaving the dressing room, one of the older skaters held out her can of hair spray to me. "Want to borrow it?" she taunted me. I felt tears stinging the back of my eyes, and I tried hard to hold them back as I made my way to the competitors' area. Suddenly I felt a hand on my arm, and Tracey was beside me.

"Don't let it get to you, Elizabeth," she whispered. "I think you look just fine. Just go out there and break a leg."

I fought to keep my concentration, but it was difficult not to be aware of the audience. I was sure they must be discussing the way I looked. The long weeks of dieting had left me weakened, and the extra weight was a definite handicap. I performed poorly, finishing in eighth position. The funny thing was, I felt a strange sense of euphoria when I came off the ice. Just knowing I could get out there, looking as I did, was a step forward. Up till this moment, I hadn't been sure I could actually do it.

The next day I skated in the long program, but from the outset I knew I wasn't on form. I made a series of glaring errors and finished in fourth position over all. Kay Thomson had retained her title as champion. I had narrowly missed a place on the world team, but I was strangely relieved not to have made it. I needed time now that this was all over to get my life back together again. Still, I was a bit hurt when a representative from the Canadian Figure Skating Association came to my hotel room soon after the competition to ask for my world team uniform back. I suppose it was needed by another skater, but the speed with which I was dropped surprised me. Giving up my uniform made my defeat so much more final, somehow.

But I was in better shape than poor Tracey, who was devastated after finishing in seventh position. She cried for a long time, and finally told me that she was going to retire. I listened sadly, knowing there was nothing I could say to change her mind. I wanted to be able to comfort her, give her my shoulder to cry on, but I was still so frightened of rejection that I couldn't seem to open up enough to give her the reassurance she needed.

My father had flown home from Germany the previous week and had come to Montreal for the championships. I hadn't seen him in a while and was excited that we would all be together again. Even though he and Mom had been divorced for some time, they had remained friendly.

When Dad saw me he could barely conceal his anxiety. He was obviously shocked by my appearance and couldn't understand how this had happened to me. Not surprisingly, he thought I wasn't taking care of myself.

Back at the hotel after dinner, an elderly lady stopped me in the corridor outside my room. "Aren't you Elizabeth Manley?" she asked. When I said yes, she asked me for my autograph. "I thought it was you," she said. "I saw you on television skating in the competition tonight."

I only just managed to get inside my room and close the door before I burst into tears. I phoned Mom's room immediately. "Oh, Mom," I wailed, "they televised my program. All those people who must have been watching, who saw me like this . . . how will I ever face anyone ever again?"

Mom came down to my room and put her arms around me while I cried. "Elizabeth — one person or one million, it isn't really any different," she said. "Most people will be rooting for you, cheering you on. You'll see."

Eventually I calmed down. "But how could CTV do that to me? They promised they wouldn't."

"I know how you feel right now," Mom said, "but you mustn't blame them. They have their job to do too. They said they would do their best, but I guess they had no choice. After all, they're paid to cover the championships. They can't leave things out."

I went back home to Ottawa, and the following weekend Mom drove down to Lake Placid to get all my stuff. Emmerich and Margie were concerned about me and told Mom I could take as long as I liked to decide what I was going to do. I should just concentrate on getting better.

My parents got together and took me to a hair specialist. It didn't take him long to diagnose my condition — I had something called *Alopecia areata*, which is hair loss caused by deep depression. He told us the weight gain was probably also caused by depression and stress.

"This is a condition that attacks thousands of women every year," he told us, "mostly young women between the ages of seventeen and twenty-five."

He spent some time examining me and asking me a battery of questions, then told me he wanted to begin a course of injections to the scalp that were designed to stimulate new hair growth. "The most vital thing for you to do now is to change the environment that seems to have produced these symptoms," he said. "*Alopecia* is caused by a variety of emotional problems — anxiety, stress, loneliness, fear, or depression. You have to create a situation for yourself that is more stable and secure."

"Will I get my hair back?" I asked, almost afraid to hear the answer.

He smiled at me. "Chances are that you will. You are young and in generally very good health. That's all I can say at this point."

"But what are the odds?" I persisted. "Can't you give me any idea at all?"

He shook his head. "I'd only be guessing. You have to be prepared that it might never grow back again." He looked at me thoughtfully. "The one thing I can tell you is that the signs are good — you haven't lost any of your body hair, and that has to be encouraging."

Earlier in the season, I had committed myself to skating an exhibition performance at a small club in Richmond, Ontario. Mom told me she would cancel it, assuming I wouldn't want to go. But I wanted to do it. I knew they were expecting me, and I didn't want to let them down. They were a great bunch of skaters, and so much fun to work with. Going there every year brought me back to reality and I always got a kick out of it.

"In that case, I am going to buy you a proper wig to wear," Mom said firmly. "At least it'll make you feel better." I protested, knowing a good wig would cost far more than Mom was able to afford, but she insisted on it.

We went into town the next morning so I could be fitted for a wig, and when we arrived at the store, we found that the hair specialist had already phoned to explain my situation. He had told them that since my remaining hair would inevitably fall out anyway, it would be better to simply shave it all off before the fitting. This way the new hair would all grow in at the same time.

I hadn't been prepared for this, and neither had Mom. Up to this point, I don't think I had ever fully accepted the fact that I was going bald, in spite of the way I looked. I had avoided thinking about it. Now I sat in a chair, watching my reflection in horror, as they shaved my entire head. I stared as the razor moved swiftly, revealing the bony outline of my skull. I was seventeen years old and I was completely bald. I started to tremble violently, then to shake, and finally the tears came, rolling down my face in rivers. For the first time I realized exactly what had happened to me. It had never seemed real before.

When I got home I started to cry all over again. Mom cried right along with me, and we clung to each other, sobbing. Finally I stopped and blew my nose furiously.

"Mom," I said, "there's something terribly wrong here. Look at me. If this is the price I have to pay for skating, then it's too high. Nothing is worth this kind of pain. When I finish the exhibition in Richmond, I'll stop. I want to give up skating."

Mom suddenly looked guilty. She always blamed herself and no matter how I protested, she continued to take everything on her own shoulders.

"I always told you that the day you wanted to quit, I would be one hundred percent behind you," Mom replied. "But I don't think you're in any condition to make a decision like that right now. Wait until you get your health back and see how you feel then. If you still want to give up at that point, then you'll know you've made the right choice."

The moment I got back from Richmond, I put my skates away. I wrote a long letter to the Danzers, telling them I wasn't coming back to Lake Placid and thanking them for their help and understanding. Margie wrote back, telling me how much they missed me. She hoped I would later change my mind. When I received that letter I realized how close to them I had grown, and how much their support had come to mean to me.

The next few weeks became the most important of my life. For so many years my hectic schedule had left no time to do anything except skate and go to school. Now I had time for self-discovery, for reflection. I spent hours thinking about my family, my friends, my career, my education. I began to understand who I was and what I wanted out of life. Each day I grew a little stronger and reached out a little further. I began to emerge from the cocoon I had lived in, and slowly hope returned.

Chapter Nine

During this time I rarely went out. I hibernated in Mom's apartment, not wanting anyone to see the way I looked. I resumed my correspondence courses to keep up with my school work and read constantly. Mom was a great comfort. I worried about the money that had been spent on my skating, feeling it had all been wasted, but she wouldn't hear a word of it. There wasn't even the slightest hint of a guilt trip. She just wanted me to be happy and healthy again. Her love was treatment in itself.

Some of the people who had seen me on television wrote to me, and I answered all the letters. Most of them were sympathetic, wishing me luck. I had a sweet note from Bob McIsaac, my friend from the Gloucester club. But many of the people I had counted as friends avoided me, and for the most part nobody called. I thought a great deal about Mark Grady and wondered if he knew I was back. We had been so close the summer before and had even spoken about getting married some day. Our parting before I left for Lake Placid had led me to believe that we would get together again as soon as I came back.

Eventually I wrote him a letter explaining what had happened to me and suggesting that he might like to come over for dinner. I waited for him to reply, but as the weeks wore on I realized he wasn't going to. I was hurt by this and went over our last meeting in my mind again and again, trying to find some reason for his silence. Much later someone told me that he had been dating another girl since Christmas. I tried to convince myself that it was all for the best, but the rejection bothered me for the longest time.

I guess it's always a painful lesson to learn who your real friends are. I had naively believed that love overcame all obstacles, but obviously that was only true of the deepest, strongest friendships. Many people avoided me during those difficult months of early 1983, perhaps because they found me an embarrassment or because they thought I was a has-been. But I treasured those who stuck by me, to cheer me on and give me courage, and I tried hard not to feel bitter toward those who didn't.

The press continued to write sporadic stories about my condition, although I avoided giving any direct interviews. One thing that upset me was the suggestion that all my problems stemmed from my parents' divorce. I always emphasized that this simply wasn't true, but the stories continued to appear. I guess it's their job to get a story, and it's always easier to write about stereotypes than about real people with complex problems.

My scalp treatments continued and the hair specialist was optimistic. I had become obsessed by my head, and each morning after I showered I would automatically examine my scalp in the mirror. One morning, early in March, I noticed the very faintest hint of fuzz showing above the skin. I screamed and called frantically for Mom. She came running, thinking there had been some terrible accident. We both stared at the almost-invisible growth, not daring to touch it. But it was real, and it kept right on growing. A hundred times a day I checked on it to make sure it was still there. I was so afraid it would all fall out again. It was a long time before I was able to stop worrying about it.

It was an exciting day when I bought my first bottle of shampoo in months. I had been using soap on my scalp and I'd even thought of writing to the makers of Dove to say that not only had their product given me a "clean, fresh face," but also one of the softest scalps in the country!

❄

One day I got a call from Marilyn Dunwoodie of the Gloucester Skating Club, asking if I would be interested in coming back to the club to work with two new coaches who were thinking of joining the teaching faculty. They were Peter and Sonya Dunfield, and they had worked with many of the top figure skaters, including Dorothy Hamill. Marilyn told me they were willing to come only if I agreed to train with them.

"But Marilyn — I can't even consider it," I protested. "I'm twenty pounds overweight, and I have no hair on my head. I'm just not ready — I've been off the ice for weeks. I'd ruin the club's chances."

"At least you could come and talk to them," she pleaded. "What harm could that do?"

"No," I said firmly. "I'm sorry. I really appreciate the suggestion, but I can't do it. I'd be too embarrassed."

Marilyn sighed. "I think you're making a mistake, Elizabeth. I want you to think about it, and I'll call you again before they come up. Maybe you'll change your mind."

As I hung up the phone, I looked at Mom in amazement. "I can't believe it," I said. "I thought everyone in the skating world had given up on me, and here are two of the top U.S. coaches offering to relocate just so they can work with me. Why on earth would they want to do that?"

"Because they know how good you are," Mom said, smiling. She could see that I was excited for the first time in months.

The invitation gave my confidence a much-needed boost. My family had always been supportive, and some of my closest friends were still there for me, but it had seemed that very few people in the skating world had even noticed I wasn't around any more. No one had phoned to see how I was. I was a figure-skating dropout, yesterday's news. And now, out of the blue, two total strangers had taken the time and trouble to seek me out and ask me to meet them. Just to know that they were even considering making such a major commitment to my career lifted my spirits.

At the end of March 1983, the World Championships were televised from Helsinki. I found myself watching avidly, following each competitor, taping all the performances and playing them over and over again. Charlene had taken my place on the Canadian team and I was happy for her — she deserved it more than anyone.

As in any pre-Olympic year, the skaters were all in top form, and I saw Torvill and Dean, the great British ice dance team, give a spectacular display of elegance and precision as they scored perfect marks for their Mack and Mabel routine. My adrenaline was pumping, and I could talk of little else at dinner that night. Mom listened, watching me in amusement.

"For someone who's given up skating, you seem to be extremely caught up in these championships," she said. "You wouldn't miss it by any chance, would you?" There was a note of seriousness underneath her teasing.

"Mom, you know how much I miss it," I said. "But I'm not sure I could go through all that again. Not any more. Besides — I told everyone that I'd thrown my skates away!"

In the middle of April, Marilyn Dunwoodie telephoned to say Peter and Sonya Dunfield were due to arrive at the club the following day. They would like an opportunity to meet with me. What had I decided to do?

It wasn't until I actually heard the words coming out of my mouth that I knew I'd made up my mind. "I'll come as long as they understand it's only to talk," I said. "I'm not in any shape to be running out to do double axels and triple salchows for them."

Marilyn assured me that they understood that and

gave me an appointment for the following afternoon. "You don't have to worry, Elizabeth," she said. "The Dunfields are aware of the problems you've been having."

I was nervous as I prepared to leave for the Gloucester club. It had suddenly become terribly important that I make a good impression, and I examined my reflection in the mirror anxiously. My head was now covered all over in a very fine red fuzz. It wasn't thick yet, nor was it more than an eighth of an inch long, but it was there and that was what counted. It certainly beat being bald.

As far as my weight was concerned, I was still twenty pounds overweight, but the worst of the bloating had disappeared, and I was no longer puffed up around my neck and shoulders. I dressed carefully and set off for the club, not quite sure why I had agreed to go.

I spent no more than an hour with the Dunfields, but in that time I found out that I wanted to work with them. I liked them both — Sonya was small, vibrant, positive, and warm; Peter, with his solid good looks and serious disposition, was quiet, intelligent, and controlled. Right from the moment I first spoke to him, I trusted him — he radiated an air of gentle and unruffled authority. Although both of them were excellent all-round teachers, Sonya was very strong on figures and Peter specialized in free skating. They seemed to be an ideal team.

I did put on my skates for a while, but they only asked me to stroke around. I'm not sure what they were looking for. Afterward, we sat in the lobby and talked for half an hour or so, and they told me they were from New York and had been working at the Sky Rink for some time. They had worked with Dorothy Hamill before she won the 1976 Olympics, and had also worked with Rosalyn Sumners and Elaine Zayak, both World and Olympic contenders. Now they were looking for someone new to train — someone with the potential to go all the way to the top.

"I don't understand why you'd be interested in me," I said. "I mean — look at me. I'm not exactly in the peak of condition!"

It was Sonya who answered, and I was touched by the warmth with which she spoke. "Elizabeth, I'm not going to tell you that we weren't a little startled when we saw you today, because that wouldn't be honest, and I want us always to be honest with each other. But the important thing is that Peter and I saw you compete in Copenhagen, and we both liked what we saw. You have a lot of drive and determination, and a special flair for free skating — the qualities it takes to make a champion. There are all sorts of things wrong with your technique, but these can be corrected. We would just like to have the opportunity to work with you if it can be arranged."

I was silent, overcome with an emotion I didn't understand. I had no idea how to reply.

Peter suddenly leaned forward and looked at me intently. "This isn't something casual we're talking about here. If we all decide to go ahead, it means Sonya and I will move to Ottawa so we can work with you on a full-time basis. It's a major commitment, and if we make it we have to know that you are willing to make the same kind of commitment to us."

"I have to tell you that I'm not really sure I want to go back into competition," I said. "I have to think it over very carefully before I give you an answer. I wouldn't want to start anything I can't follow all the way through."

Peter smiled. "Take your time and go home and talk it over with your Mom, Elizabeth. Sonya and I still have a number of other offers to weigh up before we can come to any final decision, but one way or another we'll be in touch early next week."

Long before I had reached home I knew I wanted to do it. But I was worried about what it might cost, how we would manage if we were to go back into that kind of financial situation again. Mom had just started to look relaxed for the first time in years.

In the end it was Mom who made the decision for me. When she heard what Peter and Sonya had said, she grabbed me and gave me an enormous hug. "We'll manage somehow," she said. "It's what we've been waiting for — someone who can see beyond the problems you've been having, who can look into the future and have faith in you." She opened a bottle of "bubbly" and poured us each a glass. "I think this deserves a toast."

I picked up my glass and then hesitated. "What if they don't come to Gloucester?" I asked. "Peter said they had offers from other places. Why would they want to come here, when they could probably go somewhere and work with a whole bunch of really good skaters?"

"I think they'll choose Gloucester if you are going to be there," Mom said. "I'd be ready to bet on it."

I telephoned Marilyn Dunwoodie to tell her about my decision. But I had to wait to hear whether the Dunfields would accept. As the days wore on, I became more and more anxious. I desperately wanted to finalize everything, so that the uncertainty would be over. Now that I had set my heart on a comeback, I worried constantly that the Dunfields wouldn't come. If they decided to go to another club in another city, even if they invited me to join them there, I knew I wouldn't go. Part of my attraction to this situation was that it meant I could remain at home. I couldn't face the prospect of leaving right now.

I had my answer the following Tuesday. The president of the Gloucester club phoned to say that the Dunfields had accepted their offer and were coming back from New York at the end of the week. They wanted to see me again.

When I sat down with them this time, I told them at once how much I was looking forward to getting back to work. Sonya said she was delighted, and Peter asked if I could start the following morning.

I stared at him in shock. "I can't possibly. It's too soon. I need time to lose some weight, to grow my hair back. And I have school assignments to finish up."

Peter shook his head. "No, Elizabeth. I'm not willing to accept that. Either you start immediately, or we'll just forget the whole thing."

"It'll be all right," Sonya said. "You'll see. You'll soon lose weight, and your hair is cute the way it is. Brush cuts are in this year — you're right in fashion."

"The sooner you start, the better it'll be," Peter added. "I'm staying here to work with you while Sonya goes back to New York to pack up the house."

Suddenly I found myself grinning from ear to ear. "All right," I said. "I'm game. Let's give it a try."

Chapter Ten

Working with Peter and Sonya was like starting from scratch. They were a tremendous inspiration and possessed such a vast range of knowledge. We spent days just talking and getting to know one another before I even got onto the ice.

The week that Peter was alone in Gloucester, we had an opportunity to discuss everything in the greatest detail — how I felt about competing, my attitude to skating politics, my opinions of other top skaters, my hopes and my dreams. I never once set a blade on the ice.

At the end of the week Peter told me to pack a bag. "I'm taking you to New York," he told me. "I have to go and help Sonya with the move, and we figured it would give you a chance to spend some time with us as a family. You can see us in our familiar work environment and meet our sons."

I felt very strange sitting in the car beside Peter. I was

nervous because I didn't know him very well yet, and I wondered what we would talk about all the way to New York. In the end, though, I needn't have worried. We got on like a house on fire and by the time we reached Manhattan I felt as if I'd known him for years.

It turned out to be a very good idea for me to be there with Peter and Sonya. We all got along very well and discovered that the three of us made a very powerful unit, strong enough to take on the most daunting challenges.

I stayed there three days, living in their house, eating dinner with them, helping them prepare for the move. Each day we skated at the Sky Rink, which is New York's only professional indoor rink, sixteen floors up on the top of a Manhattan office building. I watched Sonya and Peter as they worked with other students — people they would shortly be leaving behind — and I got a sense of how much they cared about everything they did.

I could tell how much Sonya was affected by the thought of pulling up her roots. She wouldn't admit it — in fact, she has never admitted it to this day — but it was plain to see that it was difficult for her to say goodbye to everybody. She reached out to me during this period; she wanted to feel close to me, but unfortunately I just couldn't provide the kind of support I felt she needed. I'm not sure why — perhaps because I was going through a major upheaval in my own life, or because I simply wasn't yet ready to open up to anyone again.

There were times, during those first months of working together at the Gloucester club, when I had doubts about getting back into the competitive world. Back into the very lifestyle I had given up as disastrous. But gradually I got over that, and I learned to trust Peter and Sonya. They took me back to the most fundamental things, the most basic techniques, and retaught me everything. It wasn't that I was doing everything wrong — it was more that I wasn't actually doing it right. Like fine-tuning, or adjusting the focus of a camera lens. Once corrected, even the smallest movement became sharper and more effective. After fifteen years of competitive skating, it was hard to believe that I had been so far off base.

The first day back in Ottawa, I was at the rink early, and I stroked around the ice for a while, warming up. I saw Sonya watching me intently from the side, and after ten minutes she called me over.

"Elizabeth, I want you to take off your skates and let me see you put them back on again," she said.

I was taken aback, but did as I was told.

Just as I was lacing up the first boot, she stopped me.

"I thought so," she said. "You've been doing it all wrong."

She showed me how to lace my boots up to the half-way point, just before the hooks start, then place my boot flat on the ground and flex my foot within it, as though I were bending my knees. This settled the foot inside the structure of the boot and ensured it would be in exactly the same position every time I wore my skates. I was astonished, because it worked. It felt better and made me feel more secure.

"It's absolutely basic to everything you do," Sonya explained. "If you wear your skates properly, you'll be consistent. It affects your technique — jumps, spins, stroking, any movement you make on the ice."

I loved working with Sonya and Peter. I couldn't wait to get out on the ice in the mornings, and each day I could feel myself improving steadily. They had so much to teach me — not just technical points, but about choreography and movement. They encouraged me to spread out and use the whole rink and they came up with unusual combinations of movements and elements for my programs.

One of the reasons our triumvirate worked so well was that Sonya and Peter had such different personalities. They brought quite distinct qualities to our relationship, and I needed them both. Sonya was a lot like me — bubbly, almost hyperactive. She was a very sensitive person, and if I didn't feel like practicing a particular jump, she would say, "It's all right, we can do it tomorrow."

Peter, on the other hand, was very tough and wasn't afraid to put his foot down when he felt it was necessary. I can be very stubborn, and Peter would yell at me sometimes. I would complain that I was tired, and he would say, "I don't care if you're tired. Just do it." I needed that. I needed someone who would take control of me and set limits for me. I guess I needed an authority figure in my life.

Of course, it wasn't always plain sailing. Sometimes I would get conflicting signals from Sonya and Peter, and I would become confused. Other times they would disagree with each other right in the middle of one of my lessons. With two such strong personalities, it was hardly surprising. But their arguments never lasted — they were devoted to each other and couldn't stay mad for long.

By June, I was back down to 108 pounds and my hair had grown into a fashionable brush cut. I was working out every day on Nautilus equipment and jogging several kilometers three times a week. On top of that, I was skating better than I had in six or seven years. Mom was thrilled by the change in me, and the summer passed in a happy whirl of hard work.

In the fall we began to prepare in earnest for the upcoming competitive season. Peter became more demanding, and I added new triple jumps to my repertoire. I'd do them over and over again, with Peter picking on seemingly endless tiny points that he felt needed to be corrected. Sometimes I would rebel, and then Sonya would say, "Trust us. It's all for a good reason." And back I would go and try again, and sure enough it would all come together in the end, I was doing triple lutzes, triple salchows, triple toe loops — and I was doing them all correctly and consistently.

One day, we were sitting in the lobby, getting our breath back, when Peter looked at me and said, "Well, I have to hand it to you, Elizabeth. You are one of the fastest learners I've ever worked with."

My jaw dropped. Nobody had ever called me a fast learner before. I had always been the one who needed more lessons than anyone else. Peter's compliment meant a lot to me. He was never one to throw around praise.

❋

The Eastern Canadian Championships were in Thornhill that December, and I won the gold medal and qualified for the Nationals. Mom was so happy as we drove back to Ottawa after the event. "It's all beginning to happen for you," she said. "All the years of hard work are starting to pay off."

I looked across at her. "It's not just me who's worked hard, Mom," I said. "If I win, it's for you too. I couldn't have done any of this without your support."

The Nationals were in Regina in January 1984, and they were one of the competitions I shall remember as long as I live. Peter and Sonya came with me, and I was absolutely ready by the time we arrived at the event. I had lost another four pounds and was the thinnest I had ever been in my life. I was glowing, partly from excitement, partly from a sense of extreme well-being. The press began to take a new interest in me. People who had known about my problems were amazed when they saw me. They couldn't believe that Elizabeth Manley was back, looking better than ever. It felt so good after all those months of living like a hermit.

I did well in the figures and came second in the short program. Going into the long program I was in fourth place, with a good chance of pulling into the medals. I landed everything, and when I spun to a stop, I saw the crowd jump to its feet, yelling its approval.

When the marks came up, I had taken the silver medal right behind Kay Thomson, and Peter started to thump me on the back. He laughed when he saw the dazed look on my face. "Don't you realize what's happened?" he asked. "You just got a place on the Olympic team!"

All I could think of was how much I wanted to tell Mom. I raced to a telephone and called her, almost in tears as I told her the news.

When I got home, Mom and I hugged each other so hard we almost stopped breathing. "Mom, I can't believe it," I said. "I'm going to represent Canada in the Olympic Games. I must be dreaming."

I had waited for so long for this moment that now it was here, I couldn't really grasp it.

I trained harder than ever over the next three weeks. Peter and Sonya prepared me mentally and physically, making certain everything was as consistent as possible. I would start at seven each morning and work on figures for a couple of hours before breakfast. Then I would free skate until noon. I would rest for an hour after lunch, then do two more hours of free skating and another hour of figures. I was under enormous pressure and every day the tension seemed to increase. Some days nothing went right and I would panic. The next day would be better and I'd calm down again. But the ups and downs added to my overall nervousness.

The press went crazy, demanding one interview after another. My Olympic uniforms arrived through the mail — all kinds of wonderful bright red garments. I tried them all on and Mom took photographs. I had costume fittings, made new music tapes, packed and repacked my cases as I tried to decide what to take. For the first time in more than a year, I even had a haircut. It was a weird feeling, sitting in the chair in the salon, knowing I had enough hair to need a trim.

Since Kay and I would be the only two from the old Rat Pack going to Sarajevo, we decided we should room together. Although we were friendly, we were also competitive and hadn't always hit it off. Kay is extremely blunt and outspoken, and I often reacted badly to the things she said. We thought it would be a good idea to try to get to know each other properly before Kay retired at the end of the season.

A few days before we left, the Gloucester club had a send-off for us. They had collected enough money to send Mom to Sarajevo with me, which was terribly exciting for her — she hadn't expected to be able to go. Under a special scheme, she was to stay with a Yugoslavian family who would bring her to the stadium every day. I knew I wouldn't get to see much of her, because the athletes live in a special village and no one else is allowed in, but just to know she would be there to experience the Olympics with me was a wonderful feeling.

Chapter Eleven

The whole Canadian Olympic team flew to Mannheim, West Germany, to train for a week prior to the Games. This gave everyone an opportunity to acclimatize to the team situation before actually confronting the Games. It was an unforgettable week, being there as part of this extraordinary group; I felt as though I were in the middle of a fairy tale.

I spent most of my time at the practice rink, and when I wasn't actually on the ice myself, I would lean over the boards and watch Brian Orser or Barbara Underhill and Paul Martini, the great Canadian pairs champions. I had the greatest admiration for Brian — I thought he was easily the best male skater I had ever seen. I was much too intimidated to speak to him, but to my amazement he came over one day and introduced himself to me. He had an outgoing and friendly personality and a very infectious grin.

We flew to Sarajevo in time for the opening ceremonies, arriving the night before. I was breathless with excitement as we waited to register, going through all the various strict security precautions to get our accreditation. I was a little unnerved when I was told that every woman on the team would have to have a mandatory "femininity" test. Apparently the use of performance-enhancing drugs and hormones produces male characteristics in female athletes, and the Olympic authorities wanted to make sure that all the women, even the ones with deep voices and facial hair, were what they said they were! The test turned out to be quite simple, they just asked for a sample of saliva, but the whole idea gave me a funny feeling.

Each country was allocated a different apartment building in the Olympic Village, but because the Canadian contingent was so large, it had two buildings to itself. Everyone on the team was there, except for the skiers; they had to stay up in the mountains, near the ski slopes. Each apartment had two bedrooms, each with twin beds, and a kitchen and bathroom. The bedrooms were neatly furnished, with beautiful blankets on the beds, covered with the fox logos that were the symbols of the 1984 Games. We got to keep these blankets, and they became the first of many treasured souvenirs I brought back to Ottawa.

The Canadian team was 80 percent male, so there were very few girls in our building. This suited Kay and me, and we decided from the outset that this was going to be a terrific experience. At eighteen, I was suddenly thrust into the middle of this athletic wonderland, with many of the world's top competitors surrounding us in the village — running, jogging, doing exercises. Kay and I just stared in awe at all these fabulous-looking men going past us. It was not easy to hang on to our concentration in such a situation!

The Ladies Figure Skating events were the last of the entire Olympic Games, so we had a week with nothing to do except practice and socialize. Unfortunately, there were only two rinks, so there simply wasn't enough ice time available to us. It had to be divided between hockey practices and games, and figure skating practices and competitions. We got only one patch per day, usually at six or seven in the morning, and one hour of free skating. Then, in the evening, we had another hour of free skating. In between, we had the whole day to ourselves with nothing to do except eat and explore the fascinating recreational distractions set up for us in the village. It was a recipe for disaster.

We would wake early — we were far too excited to sleep much, and eat breakfast before patch practice. Figure skaters are always encouraged to look their best wherever they go, and Kay and I would come down to the cafeteria all dressed up, with full makeup and our hair done. We were in sharp contrast to the speed skaters or the bobsledders, who looked like they'd just fallen out of bed, which they probably had. We were teased unmercifully about this and were always referred to as the Glamor Set.

In regular figure-skating events, we were almost invariably assigned to hotels that were close to visiting parents, coaches, judges, and members of the media. As a result, we were unlikely to get out of control. But as the Olympic Village is closed to everyone except for the athletes, it creates a very unnatural situation where everyone is thrown together, and in a very short space of time people meet and make friends in a sort of summer-camp atmosphere. At the same time, there is the under-lying tension of getting ready to compete while the whole world is watching. It's very hard to keep a sense of equilibrium, there's so much going on at once, so much to talk about, so many different emotions to deal with. The first week in Sarajevo, Kay and I had a great time, getting to know all the other athletes, hanging out in the entertainment arcade, sitting in the cafeteria drinking diet sodas and talking to everyone who came by.

I started to gain weight almost as soon as I got there. By the third day, Sonya noticed it at practice and warned me what was happening. She tried to counsel me about the dangers of too much socializing, but of course I couldn't really take it in at that point. I was having too good a time to stop. Kay and I were asked to so many parties, and we would go from apartment to apartment, talking and laughing and inevitably nib-bling on snacks. We always got to bed late.

One night we had a party in our apartment, and a group of ski jumpers came, bringing a ton of Coca-Cola with them. By the time they left, there were dozens of empty Coke cans piled up in the kitchen. One of the judges came by to see us the next morning, and she saw the cans and promptly reported to Sonya and Peter that I was devouring non-diet Coca-Colas by the dozen. I protested in vain; Peter was furious with me.

I realized toward the end of the first week that I had hardly seen anything of Mom. We made arrangements for her to come and see me practice, but of course we had forgotten that she wasn't allowed into the rink. A group of the bobsledders had become friendly with us — they were from Ottawa — and had decided to come to our practice and cheer us on. One of them, Dana Rice, noticed a little blonde woman trying to get past security and said at once, "You have to be Elizabeth's mother." He and the others, all dressed in the Day-Glo yellow tracksuits of their team uniforms and all standing about six feet tall, surrounded my Mom and swept her into the building. She had no idea who they were or what was going on, but she sat with them all through the practice and they kept her laughing the whole time. She told me afterward that she realized right then that there was no way I was going to be able to concentrate on my skating. She figured I would have to chalk this one up to experience.

Finally our competition started. I did better in the figures than I had expected, given such stiff opposition. I finished sixteenth out of twenty-three. I was terribly out of shape by this time, not only from the limited amount of practice time I'd been able to have, but also from carrying so much extra weight. Sonya was very upset about it. I skated acceptably enough in the short program, finishing seventh, and pulled up another three places to thirteenth overall. The free skating was still to come, however, and that has always been my strongest event.

That evening was the pairs free skating. Barbara Underhill and Paul Martini were strongly favored to win the gold medal and we all went to cheer them on. But during warm-up it became obvious that something was wrong with Barbara. "It's her boots," Kay told me. "She got new ones and they're not really broken in yet." Kay was right. During their program Barbara lost her footing and crashed into Paul. Their hopes were shattered and they wound up in seventh place.

When we got back to our room, Kay and I tried really hard to keep calm. It was very difficult, because everyone else had finished competing and all they were doing was celebrating and partying, so we felt we were missing out on things. We wanted so badly to go and join in.

We turned out the lights very early and lay there tossing and turning restlessly. I finally fell into a fitful sleep, only to wake again with a start at three in the morning. All the Canadians in our unit had been to watch the Canadian hockey team in its final game, and they had returned, cheering and singing. Needless to say, Kay and I were wrecks the next morning when we had to get up for practice.

I skated a disastrous long program. I knew, going in, that if I skated as well as I had in the short program, I would finish in the top ten, and this knowledge made me tense. My knees were shaking as I listened for the opening bars of Shostakovich, and I never really got the feel of the rink. My double axel was usually one of my most solid, secure jumps, and I had one planned for the opening thirty seconds of my program, but I stumbled on the landing. I never fully recovered from the blunder and felt uncomfortable for the rest of the program. In the final minute I fell on the triple toe loop and I heard the crowd groan as I went down. I knew then that I had blown my chances.

I came off the ice feeling devastated, hardly daring to

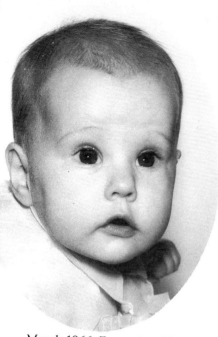

March 1966: 7 months old
and all eyes

1972: My mother and me
(bottom right), in our matching
outfits at the Trenton Figure
Skating Club

973: Greg and me, the ill-fated team

March 1973: In competition

April 1974: Competing in Montreal, aged eight,
tongue stuck firmly in cheek

April 1975: The Palestre Nationale in Montreal,
Charlene Wong in first place, myself in third place

1979: This was the year I won the gold medal at the
Eastern Ontario Sectionals in Pembroke and another gold medal at the
Divisionals in Markham

My father, myself, Tim, Greg, and Tom on my father's wedding day, 1982

Courtesy of the Canadian Figure Skating Association

Trying to look like my idol, Sonja Henie, the greatest Olympic champion of all tin

Anne Schelter, myself, and Bob McAvoy on our way
to the Senior World Championships in Copenhagen,
1982

John Santore

With Emmerich Danzer in Lake Placid, 1983

With Peter Dunfield, the coach who helped bring me back to the winner's podium

A gold medal at Moncton in the Canadian Championships in 1985, my first year as Canadian champion

Working on school figures, at first a weakness with me,
but finally one of my strengths; as of 1990 figures are no longer required in
Olympic or international competitions

February 27, 1988: The final pose of the long program; I yelled out, unable to stop myself, knowing I had skated as well as I could

Alexander Fadeev was there to wish me well
when I came off the ice

aving to the crowd with Katarina Witt and Debi Thomas: if there's a more exciting
place on earth to be than on the Olympic podium, I don't know where it is

I couldn't help biting the medal, just to remind myself that it was real and that I wouldn't wake up in the morning to find I'd dreamed it all

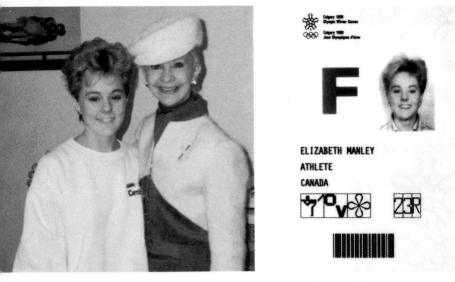

Two talismans: the photo of me with Barbara Ann Scott, who came
to wish me luck (I carried this photo around with me all night long), and my
Olympic accreditation

Mom and me at the party in Budapest
after the 1988 World Championships

With Rob McCall and Brian Orser, my best friends in the skating
world, during the I.S.U. tour

Signing the cowboy hat for the Elizabeth Manley doll,
backstage at the Ice Capades

Receiving the Order of Canada from Governor General Jeanne Sauvé

At a garden party at Rideau Hall with my brother Greg,
Prime Minister Brian Mulroney, and Mila Mulroney

Eighteen months, countless sheets of notepaper, and several ballpoint pens later,
I mail my last reply to the 3000 letters of congratulation I received after the
Calgary Olympics

Chatelaine Woman of the Year:
the January 1989 magazine cover

Paul Hendrickson and me at the
premiere party for "Dear Elizabeth,"
March 1989

With Wayne Gretzky, Janet Jones, and their baby Paulina, at the celebrity
softball match in Brantford, Ontario, June 1989

In one of my Ice Capades costumes, loving every minute of being a professional

steal a glance at Sonya and Peter. My marks were not good, to say the least, and I ended up in thirteenth place, five places behind Kay and far below the slot I had hoped for. I was bitterly disappointed with myself because I knew perfectly well I could have done so much better.

It wasn't until we got back to Ottawa that Peter sat me down and told me what he really thought about my performance at the Olympics. I was stroking around the ice at the club one morning and he called me over to the side. "Come and sit down with me, Elizabeth," he said. "I want to talk to you."

We sat in the lobby nursing steaming cups of coffee and I waited for him to tell me that they had decided to stop coaching me because of my failure.

"Elizabeth," he began, "I know how upset you are because of what happened at Sarajevo, but you must accept that what you did was anything but a disaster. You finished thirteenth, which is a very respectable place for first time out at the Olympics. Now you have to set your sights on the Worlds and forget about the past."

That was all the incentive I needed. I became determined to do better in the World Championships. I worked seven or eight hours a day, possessed by the ambition to succeed. The Worlds were to be in Ottawa, which made it even more important to me that I do well. My whole family was going to be there, and all my friends from school.

I was dating Dana Rice, a member of the Canadian bobsledding team I had met in Sarajevo. We had spent a lot of time together in the Olympic Village, and found that we had a lot in common, even though he was older than me. For the first time since I could remember, my family actually approved of one of my dates, and that made him all the more appealing. He was extremely handsome, with short dark hair and a very athletic body. I was also impressed by his degree in engineering and the black RX-7 Mazda sports car he drove. I think I was more in love with the idea of him than with the real person inside him.

❋

Just before the Worlds, Sonya took me aside to talk to me. "Don't get your hopes up too high," she warned me. "I know how much this competition means to you, but you have to remember that you're one of the new kids on the block. Politically it would be very unlikely for the judges to give you anything much higher than tenth place."

In the end, however, I placed eighth and surprised everyone. I skated a strong long program and received an enthusiastic response from the audience. I was content.

Soon after the Worlds, Dana and I broke up. I had gone to watch him play rugby one afternoon, and I stood on the sidelines, cheering and biting my nails. Afterward, he took me out for dinner and told me that he thought we shouldn't see each other any more. I was quite heartbroken. I couldn't imagine not seeing him. But we were basically too different in temperament. Dana was laid-back and passive and I was excitable and hyper. We just didn't suit each other.

By the fall, however, I had gotten over Dana and had begun to concentrate on my work again. I was to represent Canada in the NHK Trophy in Tokyo in November, and I worked hard, preparing for it. This event is sponsored by the NHK television network and is the equivalent of Skate Canada or Skate America.

I was at the rink one morning when I noticed someone leaning over the boards, applauding. It was my old friend Bob McIsaac, and I skated over to him, delighted to see him again. We began to talk and ended up having lunch together. It was great to see him. We just couldn't get all the words out we had to say to each other; they came tumbling out in a rush. I realized I had missed him, and when he asked me for a date, I accepted happily. Before long we were quite serious about each other and we spent all our free time together. Mom was upset about this, and I couldn't figure out why. I had no idea why she didn't like Bob, when she had liked Dana so much.

I went to Japan in November for the NHK competition. I was fascinated by Japanese culture, its formality and rituals, but I hated the place where the competitions were held. It was a huge frozen-over swimming pool, complete with diving boards, in a vast, gray cavernous building, where the music echoed and seemed to get lost in the rafters. The boards were very high and the audience sat a long way back from them. Skating is a lonely enough sport at the best of times, and the audience is the only company you have out there on the ice. You need that closeness. But in Tokyo I might as well have been performing at the North Pole, for all the audience response I could detect. I placed fifth, despite some stiff opposition, and Peter told me I had done very well, but I would have felt even better about it if I had been in a smaller rink with people crowding up to the boards and letting me feel their reactions to my performance.

In February 1985, the Canadian Championships were in Moncton. I skated well, but in landing the last jump of my long program, I felt a sharp pain shoot up my leg. I limped off, which obviously alarmed Peter. He was so concerned that he almost missed the announcement that I had won the gold medal. I was the Canadian champion.

When we got a doctor to look at my ankle, he told us that it was badly sprained, but he predicted that it would heal fairly quickly if I rested and didn't try to skate on it too soon. So the next day I didn't skate in the exhibitions, but I was invited to do the announcements and introductions instead, so I felt part of the proceedings.

In March I went back to Japan for the Worlds, but the ankle was still a little stiff and sore. I placed ninth, much to my disappointment. I had really wanted to do better than I had the previous year.

Mom had become very upset about Bob McIsaac. She realized that we were getting serious about each other, and she made it quite clear that she didn't approve of him. I didn't understand it at all at the time, and it caused endless scenes between us. For the first time, Mom and I seemed to have become adversaries.

Bob worked in his father's pharmacy to supplement his income from his arena work. He was paying his way through college so he could be a qualified pharmacist himself. I adored his family. His mother was a salesperson in a big department store, his brother was a university football star, and his sister was pretty and multi-talented. They lived in a great big house on the outskirts of Ottawa. I spent most of my free time there. I was rarely home any more.

Things became unbearable between Mom and me. Every time we got together, she would make some barbed comment about Bob and I would end up screaming and yelling at her. I knew it couldn't go on. It was taking its toll on us both.

The tension in my personal life showed in my skating. I found it almost impossible to concentrate, and consequently fell more often. I would lose track of what I was doing, as my mind returned again and again to my problems. Sonya made me take time off, but this didn't seem to help very much.

In June I bought new skates, hoping to give myself as long as possible before the new season to break them in. Sonya took me to Stanzione, the master boot maker in New York. He examined my feet from every angle and took a mold of each foot, so that the boots would fit me exactly. He measured me and tested my reflexes: he had so much information about my feet that I was sure the boots would fit like gloves when they were finished.

When the boots arrived, however, I almost wept. I couldn't move in them. They felt like lead weights, stiff and tight and painful. Sonya explained that this would change in time. It would be hard work to break the boots in, but once broken in, they would be the best I'd ever had. I didn't believe her at first. How I hated those boots! On top of all my other problems, this seemed like the last straw. But after two weeks, they began to feel a little less like cast iron and a little more comfortable. After four weeks, I couldn't imagine wearing any other kind of boots.

Chapter Twelve

Around the beginning of 1986, I met a group of girls who had rented a house. They were looking for someone to take a spare bedroom that was empty because one of them had left to get married. They were all university students, and I was intrigued. I thought I would like to live with people who knew almost nothing about figure skating. I asked if I could move in with them and they told me they would love to have me.

The hardest thing I have ever had to do was to tell Mom about moving out of the apartment. She was devastated. She figured it was Bob's fault — that he had talked me into it. But really it had nothing to do with him. It was my own need for independence and privacy. After all, I was twenty, an age when lots of kids have already left home. I knew I needed to learn to be more independent if I was to make it as a professional skater.

"Mom, please try to understand," I begged. "I have to do this. We can't go on fighting the way we are. We just need some time apart, that's all."

Mom was not to be consoled. She wept at first, but later she became bitter. "We've been through so much," she cried. "How can you let Bob talk you into something like this?" She couldn't seem to understand that it was my own idea.

My room was in a townhouse in a suburb of Ottawa. The only furniture I had was a bed and a chest of drawers, but I loved it. We shared the cooking and the chores and I enjoyed the casual relationships with the other girls. No one would interfere with anyone else's affairs, but there was always someone to talk to. There were four of us there, but we'd often have a guest for a few days. It was never dull. We had parties and dinners, and sat around talking about everything under the sun. The funny thing was, I grew more mature in this environment. I was now responsible, not only for my share of the house duties, but also for my own life. Mom wasn't there for me with meals, clean laundry, or the extra ten dollars I needed at the last moment. I had to manage on my own and I found I was good at it. And since I knew that one day I would want to tour with an ice show, I felt that the experience would be invaluable. I got to bed earlier than ever before and was never late for practice. I ate properly and took better care of myself. Peter and Sonya, who had originally been dubious about the arrangement, had to admit that it was working out fine.

Mom and I couldn't seem to bridge our differences that year. I would visit her, but inevitably she would start to criticize Bob and I would leave in a terrible mood. We said hurtful things to each other, and for a while I worried that the bond we had shared for so long was broken forever.

I went to North Bay for the Canadian Championships in 1986. It was February and I was still in turmoil over my relationship with Bob and my having moved out of the apartment. It wasn't the most promising state of mind to be in. I came second, losing the title to Tracey Wainman, who had just made a dramatic comeback. Sonya and Peter were upset, not because I hadn't skated well — they thought I had done extremely well — but because they felt I should have won the title. They felt that my position had been affected by the excitement over Tracey's return. The press dismissed my performance and I read some discouraging things about myself in the papers.

※

I had started to work with a wonderful sports psychologist named Peter Jensen. He helped many members of the Canadian Olympic team, and he was a particular favorite of Peter and Sonya. He taught me his technique of visualization, which enables you to visualize the perfect program in your head. You have to concentrate really hard, going over and over the elements and the choreography. Some people visualize as if they were outside, watching themselves do the program. Others visualize from the inside, experiencing the routine as they perform it. I found the former method to be more rewarding.

Many young skaters think this visualization technique is a fantasy — that there is no real value to it at all. I suppose I was skeptical about it at first myself. But now I know better. It works wonders. If I had been exposed to it a few years earlier, I might have been a world champion. I truly believe that. The difference between winning and losing is more often mental than physical.

The week before we left for the 1986 World Championships in Geneva, I went to bed early every night and thought about my program, going through every detail, every jump, every spin. I went over and over it, hearing the music of Prokofiev and Falla in my mind, until I could see myself doing it perfectly. Sonya told me to trust this method — she had seen it work for others. I believed because she believed. And after all, I had nothing to lose.

Geneva was remarkable for a number of reasons. Our stay began with a very funny incident. The team had received a number of freebies from various sponsors, and these included a particular brand of cough drop from a Canadian manufacturer. Shortly after we arrived, the representative of the Canadian Figure Skating Association somehow learned that these cough drops contained some substance that was prohibited by drug-testing regulations. He tore around the hotel, beating on our doors, and grabbing back the cough drops, terrified that we might accidentally disqualify ourselves by eating one.

Drug testing is very strict for figure skaters, so chances are that even if I'd had a cough, it wouldn't have occurred to me to take a cough drop. I never even took painkillers for headaches or medication for colds because we were tested so often. I usually found the testing a nuisance. After all, I would be in and out of the bathroom a hundred times before I performed, then I would sweat buckets when I was out on the ice, and I would come back, dehydrated, only to be asked for two bottles of urine. I have no idea why they need so much, but it meant that we'd be swigging beer in the drug-testing room just to provide a specimen. Even then, when one of the women officials who conducted the drug testing actually followed me into the cubicle, it was all I could do to produce a drop, let alone two bottles full.

The day of the long performance at Geneva, I drove to the arena in a van with Peter Dunfield, Jill Trenary, her coach, Carlo Fossi, and his wife. Just as we turned into the parking lot, the van stopped suddenly and someone threw a coat over my head. For one wild second I wondered if we'd been hijacked. Then the van started to move and I pulled off the coat.

"What happened there?" I asked Carlo, who was sitting beside me.

"I'm sorry about that," he explained. "I threw the coat over you because there was an ugly accident right there, in front of the van. Some poor man on a bicycle was hit, I think he may be dead, and I didn't want you to see it."

I was a bit shaken, but grateful to Carlo for his quick thinking. I was also surprised that he would have such consideration for somebody else's student.

That night I skated an almost perfect long program. I found myself doing exactly as I had imagined in my visualizing efforts, skating the best I have ever skated in my life. Fortunately, Peter caught my performance on videotape, and afterwards I was able to use the tape to help when I wanted to visualize the perfect triple.

I finished in third place in the combined free-skating segments, and fifth over all. Debi Thomas of the U.S. took the championship. To my utter amazement I was invited to join the International Skating Union tour of Europe along with the top medalists. We would be performing in all the major European capitals. I was ecstatic.

I felt like a real rookie on that I.S.U. tour. I formed close friendships with Brian Orser and with Rob McCall, the Canadian ice-dance champion who worked with Tracy Wilson, and the three of us did everything together. We had so much fun. We partied and ate in wonderful little restaurants and even went skiing in France. It was the first time I'd ever gone skiing in my life. I was cautious though, and hired an instructor for the day. My legs are my career, and I knew I had to take care not to break anything. A day of fun on the ski slopes is not worth a lifetime's work.

Paris was such a romantic city. I loved it. I looked out of my hotel window at the lights and couldn't believe I was actually there. We had only two days in Paris. By the time we had rehearsed and done the show on the first night, it was already late. Back at the hotel, as I was walking down the corridor, I stopped by an open door. I could see two of the top Soviet skaters inside the room, talking animatedly, Victor Petrenko and Aleksandr Fadeev, who had won the men's world title in 1985. On an impulse, I went inside and started chatting with them. They spoke some English, but we had to resort to sign language at times, and we found ourselves laughing hysterically at our own efforts to communicate. I was inexplicably drawn to Aleksandr, in a way I had rarely experienced before. It was quite different from the way I had been drawn to Bob or to Dana. I could tell he felt it too. We stayed talking for the rest of the evening and far into the night. I finally crawled into my bed at five in the morning, exhausted but happy. I knew I had found someone very special in Aleksandr. There was also an exciting element of the forbidden in befriending someone from a Communist country that I found irresistible.

At nine in the morning I heard someone banging on my door. I tried to block out the noise, and when it continued I shouted to whoever it was to go away. I was so tired and all I wanted to do was sleep. But the banging continued until I was forced to get out of bed and open the door. Outside was Brian Orser.

"Come on, sleepyhead," he said. "Time to get up and do some sightseeing."

"No way," I groaned and crawled back to bed, pulling the covers over my head.

He yanked them off again. "No, Elizabeth. This is Paris, remember? I refuse to let you sleep the day away. Take a shower — you'll feel better."

So in the end, that's what I did. I ran cold water over my head and dressed. Then Brian and I went to a little outdoor cafe and had a breakfast of croissants and rich French coffee. I began to feel better.

That was quite a day. We went to the Eiffel Tower, Notre Dame, and all the famous landmarks. As we ate lunch and I took my thousandth photograph of Brian posed against the Paris skyline, he grinned at me. "See what you'd have missed if I hadn't taken the trouble to wake you up?"

I had to admit he was right. I had so much fun with him, and we became better friends that day. It was the beginning of a friendship that would take us through many similar tours and would provide us with some very special memories.

I saw Aleksandr again that evening and we talked openly about our feelings for each other. Neither of us had ever experienced an attraction quite like this before, and we didn't quite understand it.

"It is sad. We are from different cultures," Aleksandr said. "I think it cannot work for us to be together."

I didn't say anything. I knew he was right.

"I must go back to the Soviet Union and be married. To girl I know for long time. She is daughter of family I live with."

I felt a lump in my throat. "Do you love her?" I asked.

"What is this love? She is my friend. She will be my wife and we will make a family together. That is enough." He paused. "Yes, I love her. Not how I feel for you. But, yes, I love."

I found myself telling him about Bob, about how we had discussed marriage and how I felt about him. I told him Bob was the most important person in my life. "Can you understand that, Aleksandr? How I can love him and still feel as I do about you?"

"Yes," he answered. "I understand. I feel same."

He put his arm around me and we walked slowly through the darkened Paris streets in friendly silence. It was dawn before we finally said goodbye.

❄

When I got back to Ottawa I continued to see Bob for the rest of the summer. We took it for granted that we would marry. We talked about the children we would have, where we would live, what we would do. We rarely went out anywhere. I was always too tired at the end of the day, because I was working hard at the rink. We usually just went home and talked or watched television until it was time for Bob to leave. Some nights I would go to his house and have dinner with his family. I always loved those occasions, and they were the times I felt closest to Bob. I appreciated the way he accepted my career — his unquestioning support and encouragement. I felt safe and unpressured with him.

Mom insisted that I didn't really love Bob. She figured I was in love with his family, with the security they offered. I always hated it when she said things like this and I'd deny it vehemently, telling her to shut up and mind her own business. I often ended up slamming out of the apartment. After one of these exchanges I'd feel miserable and guilty for days. I believed Mom was jealous of Bob's family and frustrated that she wasn't able to provide the same environment. If only she had realized that no one else could have come close to giving me the kind of love she had always given me.

For her part, Mom believed that I would be making a terrible mistake if I married Bob. "You're too inexperienced to marry yet," she would say. "He's the wrong person for you. I wish you would listen to me before it's too late."

Dad and Betty had been transferred back to Ottawa.

He soon discovered that Mom didn't like Bob and he immediately decided that he was going to encourage the relationship. He invited us over to dinner and told us that he thought we were perfectly suited. I realized for the first time that Dad was trying to reach me, believing he would have to break into the bond that I had with Mom. I tried to show him that I loved him for himself and that it had nothing to do with my relationship with Mom.

Some nights I would tell Bob that I couldn't see him because I had to go to Mom's, and then he would complain bitterly. "Why can't I go with you? If we're going to be married, your Mom is going to have to accept me." But I knew she wouldn't, so I continued to visit her alone, resenting the fact that this was necessary. My nerves were growing raw under the strain.

I went to London in the fall of 1986 to skate in the St. Ivel championship, the British equivalent of Skate Canada or Skate America. I won the gold medal, which made a good impression on the Canadian Figure Skating Association. I was receiving $10,000 from them for the 1986-87 skating season, and I wanted them to feel that I had justified their faith in me.

One of the things Mom and I didn't quarrel about was money. I worried constantly about the pressures the skating costs had placed on her, and she always made it clear to me that it was something she had chosen to take on. She insisted that I wasn't to worry about it. However, I wanted to try to find a sponsor for myself, to take some of the expenses off her shoulders. I knew other skaters had them, yet I had no idea how to go about securing one. I knew I couldn't get any kind of commercial sponsorship, as skaters are forbidden to advertise products (such as by wearing a certain brand of sports-wear with a prominent logo on it in competition) but I was aware that sometimes clubs or wealthy individuals were prepared to sponsor skaters and help them with the expenses of competitions. I had always hoped that someone would approach me with an offer of sponsor-ship, but it didn't happen. Still, I now had an A-card from Sport Canada, which meant that I ranked with the top eight in my sport world-wide and entitled me to an additional $7800 a year, on top of what I received from the association.

Amateur skaters are not allowed to earn money for their ice performances, nor for their skill or fame as a skater. In Communist countries this has always been a farce, since top amateur athletes are treated like stars and live in relative luxury. Also, nowadays many skaters sign with agents and managers before turning profes-sional and are allowed to earn substantial sums of money that are placed in trust accounts for them until they turn professional. I have never understood the point of this. After all, they are earning money from their skill and fame as skaters, and the money is theirs, even if they have to wait to use it. It all seems a little hypocritical, somehow. It seems to make the concept of amateur status obsolete.

❄

Peter and Sonya put a new program together for me for the 1987 competitive season. It placed a greater empha-sis than ever on the choreography, using my love of line to more advantage. We took a long time to learn the program, working for only about half an hour at a time. Sonya had long since discovered that I had a short attention span, and that I needed to take regular breaks. In the end, I learned much more quickly this way.

Peter and Sonya taught me the most valuable thing of all that winter — they completely changed my attitude toward school figures. I had always looked on figures as something loathsome, something quite extraneous that took up time I could have been spending on free skating. But Peter and Sonya taught me that free skating and figures were inextricably interwoven, that one could not exist without the other. Great free skating is a natural expansion of figures — the greater the technique, the greater the potential for artistry. So I learned a new respect for school figures and no longer balked at doing three or four patches a day. I realized that figures are as important to free skating as scales are to the playing of a great concerto.

I didn't find an actual sponsor, but I got a wonderful surprise. Dad belonged to a sports club in Ottawa, where men would get together and watch sports on television, talk, and drink. One day Dad told me that Gordie Hamilton, the man who ran the club, had talked a group of the members into leasing a car for me to use until after the 1988 Olympics. Gordie had been a friend for years, always taking time to chat and joke with me. He was one of my first real adult friends. I was overwhelmed by his generosity, because it was the first time anyone had ever given me anything like that. Up to this point, I had been spending three or four hours a day on buses, traveling back and forth to the arena. Bob had been as helpful as he could, driving me to costume fittings and often taking me home in the evenings. But having my own set of wheels made a tremendous difference. I'm not sure I could have made it all the way to the Olympics without that car, so I owe Gordie a great debt of gratitude.

Betty also gave me a lot of help. As a dietitian and nutritionist for the Armed Forces, she knew all about meal planning and weight control, and she appointed herself my personal nutritionist. She weighed me once a week and gave me menu suggestions and food ideas which I found very helpful. It gave me that little bit of extra discipline that I needed to keep my weight under control and eat healthily.

Bob and I were beginning to have terrible fights. I suppose it was inevitable, given the odds we were battling. All the same, these scenes shook me up and left me feeling depressed. I had opened up to Bob so completely; he knew more about me than anyone else. I had shared everything with him, even my most intimate secrets. Now we were saying hurtful things to each other, accusing each other of being destructive or possessive. For the first time, he was beginning to resent my heavy schedule, and in an effort to bring peace and harmony back to our relationship I turned down invitations to perform or to make public appearances, which I really should have accepted. As the weeks went by, I began to realize that we were heading for a split.

It was hard to grasp how we could be so much in love and still be tearing each other apart. Of course, this situation was exactly what Mom had predicted, and I saw now that she had been right all along. I remem-

bered the old axiom about love and athletics not mix-
ing. When I was away from Bob, I could see his point of
view, and I knew he deserved a better relationship than I
could give him, but I couldn't bring myself to let go.

Chapter Thirteen

In February 1987, the Canadian Championships were held in Ottawa. This was terrific for me, because I didn't have to leave home to compete. My whole family was planning to attend the event, which made it extra special — Dad hadn't seen me skate since I had started working with Sonya and Peter, and I was eager to show him how far I had come.

Sonya and Peter arranged extra ice time for practice, and I worked long hours, making sure that everything was as secure as possible. We worked extra hard on my double axel. "Hold the landing," Peter would shout. "Hold it, hold it — *longer!* Back I would go and try again and he would remind me to get my head up high and watch my entry. Finally he would be satisfied and I would collapse on to a bench at the side of the ice to get my breath back.

Just before we drove to the arena for the compulsory

figures, Peter looked at me and said, "Elizabeth, this is the moment to take your title back. You can do it. Your figures are there, your programs are right, and you're prepared. Just go out there today and remember all the things we've discovered." He hugged me, and I felt a surge of confidence that stayed with me all the way through the competition. I skated much better than usual in the figures and went on to recapture my title. I was the Canadian champion again and suddenly I was looked on as having an outside chance at the World title.

Early in March, I finally broke up with Bob. It was difficult for us to part, but it was the only thing we could do. We were always fighting, often over trivial things, silly incidents that blew up into monumental battles that left us dazed from the bitterness with which we fought. We loved each other, but we could not seem to be in the same room together without fighting. When we decided to break up, and realized what it meant, we both felt torn and miserable. Part of me couldn't believe we could actually go through with it. But we had no choice.

The Worlds were in Cincinnati that year, and I was told by David Dore, the director general of the Canadian Figure Skating Association, that I was expected to win. The press were behind me again, and I received a deluge of mail wishing me well. My chief rivals were considered to be Debi Thomas, the reigning world champion from the United States, and Katarina Witt, the East German skater. Katarina had won the gold medal at the 1984 Olympics and had far more experience than I did, but I was ready to take her on — in fact, I couldn't wait to get started.

As soon as I arrived in Cincinnati, I looked everywhere, hoping to catch a glimpse of Aleksandr. We usually saw each other at the opening draw, but I was late this year and I missed it. We had made a pact that we wouldn't communicate with each other until we had finished competing, but I wanted so much just to see his face and to reassure myself that he was real. Right now I needed to be close to him, even if he didn't know I was there.

When the men's competition began, I decided to sneak into the back of the arena to watch the compulsory phase. I knew Aleksandr was in first place after the initial figures, and I arrived just as the second one was beginning. He was on the ice, warming up, when I slid into one of the empty seats near the entrance. I sat down quietly and watched him making perfect circles, his head bent toward the ice in complete concentration. I felt my heart lift, as it always did when I saw him, and I leaned forward to see him better. Just as I did so, he looked up and caught sight of me, and he smiled slightly. He looked away quickly, because he didn't dare acknowledge me for fear of upsetting the Russian team coach. I swallowed hard. I wasn't sure what to do — I knew I was having a bad effect on him because I had broken his concentration. He was clearly fighting to regain it. The whole time he was tracing his figure eight he kept glancing over at me. I could see that the coach was beginning to get uptight, wondering what was going on. He was a new coach, and he didn't know me. I decided to leave, got up, and made my way to the end of the row of seats.

David Dore and Marilyn Dunwoodie, the 1987 Canadian team leader, were standing in the aisle, and as I approached them, they turned to me.

"Why don't you stay?" Marilyn asked.

"I can't, Marilyn," I said. "I have to go and get a cup of coffee until Aleksandr is finished. I think I'm affecting his concentration."

"That's his problem, not yours," said David Dore. "There's no reason why you shouldn't watch if you want to."

I walked a few paces down the steps with them and stood uncertainly for a couple of moments, watching. Just then, Aleksandr moved out and took up his axis, ready to compete. One of the judges came forward and said, "Mr. Fadeev, it's not your turn yet."

Aleksandr looked confused and returned to the practice area. I saw his coach speaking to him with a frown on his face.

I sat down in one of the seats, not at all sure what to do, feeling that this would be less conspicuous than if I walked out. I clenched and unclenched my hands nervously, convinced that I had jinxed Aleksandr.

A few minutes later he skated back to the judging area, took up his axis again, drew a deep breath, and began to skate. He did a perfect bracket and won the figure by a large margin. Under my breath I was saying, "Thank you, God," because although I supported my own team, I wanted Aleksandr to do well in the competition.

I didn't see him again until after the men's event was finished. He won the bronze medal, behind Brian Boitano and Brian Orser, and came to watch my free skate practice. He didn't speak to me, nor did he look at me directly. He just brushed past me, reaching out to touch my arm briefly as he went. Then he climbed the stairs and sat down.

I was conscious of his eyes following my every move on the ice, but far from making me nervous, it inspired me. I had a phenomenal practice. I was flying all over the ice, using the visualization technique Peter Jensen had taught me. As I came off at the end of the session, I caught sight of Aleksandr leaving the building, and he turned around and waved briefly. I wanted to run after him and give him a big hug.

Peter took me for a cup of tea, and we sat and discussed the short program that afternoon and how I should approach it. He said he was very happy with the way I had practiced and that he felt I was as prepared now as I would ever be. As I was leaving to go back to the hotel for a rest, he put an arm around me. "You've come such a long way," he said, smiling. "It's all about to pay off."

I knew it would be disastrous for me to look for Aleksandr. I couldn't simply say hello and walk away again. I needed to be calm and to prepare myself for the afternoon's program. I walked back to the hotel, and as I was crossing the lobby, I saw Toller Cranston, the 1976 bronze medalist, who was in Cincinnati covering the Worlds for Canadian television. He stopped me and planted a kiss on my cheek. "That's for luck, Lilibets. I know you can do it," he said.

I won the short program, skating to music from *The Fantasticks*. I landed everything, and when I had finished, Peter hugged me and told me he was very proud of me. I had beaten Katarina Witt and Debi Thomas. It was hard to stop my pulse racing.

I met Tracy Wilson, who skated pairs with Rob McCall, for dinner later. We ate in the hotel coffee shop, in the back of the room where it was quiet. I ate lightly, an omelet and a salad. My weight was just right and I was being very careful. Tracy looked at me as we sat sipping our tea.

"What would you do if Aleksandr showed up on your doorstep one day, saying he'd defected?" she asked.

I wasn't startled by the question. It was one I had often asked myself and something I knew Mom worried about continually. Without hesitation I told her, "I'd marry him."

She shook her head. "That's what we all figured. But Elizabeth — you'd have to stop and think before you did something like that. I mean, I know how attracted you guys are to each other, but there are so many underlying differences — religion, culture, language. It would all be so difficult."

"I know," I said. "But Aleksandr and I have talked about it, and he's told me that he could never leave the Soviet Union, so there's not much point in worrying about it. And I can't really see myself living in the Soviet Union."

❄

The next day I had such an inspired practice that Peter pulled me off the ice after twenty minutes. "Everything's too good," he said. "Better save it for tonight."

I walked with Sonya back to the hotel and she chattered enthusiastically about the upcoming competition. She was bubbly, as she always is, and I could feel her energy affecting me. By the time we reached the hotel, I felt as though I had consumed a massive dose of caffeine. It took me a long time to calm down again.

Mom and I had lunch together. She had come to Cincinnati with me, and we found we got on much better than we had in a long time. We didn't mention Bob and tried to keep the conversation light and easy. Mom had always had a steadying influence on me and could take my mind off things that were bothering me. We hugged as we parted, and Mom told me she was sorry things had been so rough between us lately. I told her I was sorry too and that we would try to work it out when we got back home.

I bought all the newspapers after lunch and took them to my room to read. Big mistake. As soon as I opened them I realized that I had been adopted as the new hot ticket for the title, and my picture appeared on many of the sports pages. I phoned Peter to tell him, and he warned me not to think about it, to empty my mind of all the hype that was going on. I tried, but it was difficult.

Finally the evening came. I hadn't seen Aleksandr at all and was feeling relatively relaxed. I dressed carefully, and Peter took me to the arena half an hour before I was due to warm up. I sat down and tried to visualize the program, but I couldn't seem to do this as successfully as I usually did. At nine-twenty, the long program competition began.

As we warmed up, Katarina studiously avoided me, but Debi slapped me on the back and wished me luck. I was very keyed up — adrenaline was pumping furiously through my body. Everything tingled, anticipating the moment when I would be able to go out and do my

147

program. I wanted to prove myself — finally and irrevocably — to all those people who had given up on me and to the press. I also wanted to prove myself to my family and friends, who had had to put up with so much over the years.

When my name was called, I skated to center ice and stood, waiting for the first notes of "The Night They Invented Champagne" from the musical *Gigi*. I fought to concentrate on the program ahead of me, but my mind kept slipping out of focus. I was much too aware of the audience all around the arena. At last the tape began, and I launched into my routine, a few seconds behind the music. I could feel myself slipping further and further back, and I struggled to stay in synch. I was only a minute into the performance when I knew I wasn't going to make it. Something was wrong and I couldn't seem to hold on. I fell several times and as I finished my final spin I had to fight to keep the tears back. I had to get off the ice before that happened. I couldn't cry in front of seventeen thousand people.

Peter and Sonya rushed over to me, but I couldn't look at them. I stared straight ahead, forcing myself to keep calm. Inside, I felt sick. I had blown away the best chance I had ever had to become the world champion, and I simply had no idea what was wrong.

I waited in the "kiss and cry" area where competitors watch for their marks. When the marks for technical merit came up, they were abysmal. Suddenly I couldn't sit there any longer and wait for the artistic marks. I was close to breaking down, and I wanted to get away before I did. I excused myself and pushed past Peter and Sonya.

I ran from the arena and didn't stop until I was inside the dressing room.

I collapsed on to one of the benches and began to sob. I don't think I've ever cried so hard in my life. I felt as though I was turning inside out. Everything was ruined and I didn't think anything would ever work out for me again.

Suddenly I felt an arm around me and I looked up to see Toller. He held me for a minute, rocking me slightly. "Elizabeth," he said, "you have to pull yourself together. You have to go back out there and show yourself. You can't run out on everyone, no matter what has happened."

"I can't," I wailed. "I just want to die. You don't know how I feel."

"Oh yes, I do," he said. "I know exactly how you feel. A long time ago, in Vancouver, I was in the same situation. I had a very upsetting experience and I ran away to the dressing room, just the way you did. And my coach, Ellen Burka, cared enough to come after me and make me go back out again. She told me that if I didn't, I would never get over it. Now it's your turn. You have to go out there and face it. You have to talk about it. Trust me, it won't feel so bad once you've done that."

He steered me over to the washbasin, and I dabbed my face with cold water. I held my breath, trying to stem the sobs, and gradually they subsided into hiccups. I looked in the mirror and saw my red, swollen eyes and the streaks where the tears had run down my face.

"I can't go on camera looking like this," I said. "I'm a mess."

Toller patted me on the back and pushed me gently ahead of him. "Come on," he said. "Let's go."

I turned just before we reached the television area and put a hand on his arm. "By the way," I whispered, "where did I finish?"

"You finished fourth," Toller told me. "Katarina got her title back from Debi."

"Who was third?"

"Caryn Kadavy."

I swallowed hard. Caryn was the third-ranked U.S. competitor, and she had taken the bronze medal.

When we were standing inside the television interview area, Toller put his arm around me and looked directly into the camera. "No matter what's happened here tonight," he said, "Elizabeth Manley is still the best female skater there is. She can learn from this experience, and when she goes to Calgary next year for the Olympics, she will be stronger than ever. Just watch her."

I started to cry again. I couldn't help it. Here was Toller Cranston, a man I had admired for years, saying these things to the entire country. I turned to smile at him and saw a tear trickling slowly down his nose. That choked me up completely, and when I opened my mouth to speak, I couldn't say anything. All I could do was turn to the camera and give a big thumbs-up sign.

Chapter Fourteen

I left the television area as soon as possible, anxious to get back to the sanctuary of my hotel room. I told Peter and Sonya that I would see them early the next morning, to prepare for the afternoon's exhibitions. Mom asked me to have supper with her, but I couldn't do it. "I need to be by myself," I explained. "Please try to understand." She hugged me and told me to call her if I changed my mind.

When I was finally inside the hotel room, I closed the door, lay down on the bed, and began to cry again. I cried for hours until I was exhausted.

I must have fallen asleep at some point, because I was awakened at one in the morning by a soft, persistent tapping at my door. I got up, still half-asleep, and opened it.

Aleksandr stood outside, smiling shyly, and I gasped. He was the only person I wanted to see and I had been praying he would come. Without saying a word, he opened his coat to reveal two plastic hotel glasses and a bottle of gin that he had concealed in his inside pocket. He knew I rarely drank, but that when I did, I liked gin and tonic.

"Antoushka," he said as he stepped inside, "I come to solve your problems."

Aleksandr had christened me Antoushka from the moment we had first met. "Like cartoon person," he had explained. "In Russia, Antoushka is cartoon everyone love." The name had stuck, and now everyone on the Soviet team called me Antoushka. I called Aleksandr Sniffles, because when I first met him he had been nursing a terrible cold. We used the names not only to show affection for each other, but also to confuse the authorities. Our friendship had been noticed by Aleksandr's coaches, and it had been actively discouraged.

Ever since the legendary Protopopovs, the great Russian pairs champions, had defected in the late 1970s, the authorities kept a close watch on the Russian skaters. If they had understood Aleksandr's devotion to his motherland, however, they wouldn't have worried. Aleksandr had always made it perfectly clear that he would never consider leaving the Soviet Union to be with me.

There was another reason why Aleksandr could not enjoy an open relationship with me, and that was his recent marriage. This was more or less an arranged marriage that had been inevitable for a long time. Some years back he had been sent to Leningrad to train with the Red Army, and he had been boarded with a family of synchronized swimmers. He had lived there for a number of years, and it became understood that he would marry their daughter. I think what he was looking for at the time he met me was someone to reach out to as a friend. Neither of us had intended to get as involved as we had.

Since we had met in Paris, we had kept in touch by letter, and our feelings for each other had grown. Suddenly, that night in my hotel room, we were swept away by emotion. We clung to each other, and Aleksandr murmured my name over and over.

Finally we broke apart and Aleksandr sat me down on the sofa beside him. With one arm still around me, he used his free hand to pour out two shots of neat gin.

"Where's the tonic?" I asked.

"Is no tonic," he said. "Is better this way."

I sipped it and it scalded my throat and exploded inside my empty stomach. I felt a glow travel up toward my head and right away I felt infinitely more relaxed.

Aleksandr lifted his glass to me. "To Antoushka," he said, "the most beautiful girl in whole world. And best skater." He leaned over and kissed me gently. Suddenly I knew that nothing else mattered at that moment except that we were together.

At one point, Aleksandr tried to explain to me how he felt about his wife, and how it was that he could love us both. I saw tears in his eyes as he struggled to find the words. I stopped him.

"I understand what you are trying to say," I told him. "Believe me, I know exactly. I feel the same way about Bob. I love him, but I love you too, in quite a different way."

Aleksandr looked at me gratefully. "Good. Then we share this, Antoushka. We keep this night in our hearts. To remember, when we go home."

❋

I was invited to go on the tour that followed the Cincinnati Worlds. I was thrilled, because it meant that Aleksandr and I would have more time together.

Before we left, I had a long talk with Peter about my future. He wanted me to understand that although my fourth-place finish was going to hurt my chances in the Olympics the next year, it was by no means the kiss of death.

"Politically it's very unfortunate," he said. "But you've always been a fighter. You can come from behind and make it work for you. You just have to try even harder."

I assured him that I wasn't about to give up without a fight, and he grinned at me.

"That's my girl — that's the Elizabeth I was hoping to hear. You go off and enjoy the tour and I'll see you when you get back to Ottawa."

I loved the I.S.U. tour. Tommy Collins, who produced these tours, is one of my favorite people, and he always worked extra hard to make sure everything on those tours was perfect. He treated us like royalty. Every audience was enthusiastic, every hotel was first class, every meal was delicious. We never had to haul around our own luggage and we had buses to take us to the arena each night. There were receptions and special entertainment laid on in many places. We didn't get paid much for skating these shows — the Canadian Figure Skating Association wouldn't allow us to receive anything but a small stipend — but it was still money, and I was glad that I would be able to give something to Mom when I got back.

Aleksandr and I were together every moment we could get away, but for a lot of the tour I hung around with Rob McCall and Brian Orser. I was happy with them. The three of us got on very well, and when I wanted to spend time with Aleksandr, they often covered for me.

One night, when we were in Los Angeles, we were invited to La Cage aux Folles nightclub after the show. One of the waiters had seen me on television and he made a huge fuss over me. I could see Aleksandr getting irritated by this, but when the waiter followed us back to the hotel after dinner, I wasn't prepared for the jealous rage that gripped Aleksandr. He almost threw the boy down the hotel steps. Then he grabbed me roughly by the arm and hustled me into the hotel elevator. It wasn't until we were inside my room that he let go of me. He stood there, breathing heavily, his eyes blazing.

I was furious. I had never experienced anything like that before, and I felt humiliated. "How could you do that?" I demanded. "You're the one who's married, not me. I haven't done anything wrong."

As soon as the words were out, I wished I hadn't said them. I saw the pain in his eyes and knew he hadn't meant to hurt me. He held out his arms and I walked into them. We stood there for a long time, my face against his chest, where I could hear his heart pounding.

"Antoushka," he whispered. "I love you so much. What will we do?"

"I don't know," I answered miserably.

At that moment, if he had asked me to come back to the Soviet Union with him, I would have done it. Fortunately for us both, he didn't.

At the end of the tour, Aleksandr and I shared a quiet dinner at a little restaurant in New York. We knew it would be our last opportunity to see each other for a long time, and both of us were sad.

"Antoushka," he said as we prepared to leave, "remember always that I love you. Is in my heart. This will never change."

❋

Back in Ottawa, I saw Bob again and we agreed that we couldn't make a go of it. This time we had broken up for good. I knew that we could never recapture the closeness we had once shared. What I didn't admit — even to myself — was how much my relationship with Aleksandr had affected my feelings for Bob. I didn't want to think about it.

At the same time, I knew that Mom was not to blame for what was happening. She had been genuinely worried about my intention to marry Bob. She felt that a marriage between us wouldn't have worked out, and I had to admit that she was probably right. My lifestyle was a great deterrent. Mom knew I had to marry someone who understood that I had to travel and perform. Someone who was in the same business. She felt that Bob was too sedentary. I finally understood that she had been trying to protect me and that I had made this very difficult for her. Much as I hated to do it, I admitted to her that I had been wrong, and we made up.

I decided to find a bachelor apartment close to Mom's place. I felt this would be the ideal solution for the Olympic year. I would be close to her, but I would still have my privacy, which had become very important to me. Because I had my A-card from Sport Canada, I could just afford the rent.

I looked at a couple of places the next day and found one I really loved right in Mom's building. I rented it immediately and moved in on the weekend. I didn't have much furniture — just a bed, a chest of drawers, and a television set — but it had its own bathroom and a kitchen built into the wall. It was the size of a large broom closet, but it was my own, and that was what mattered to me.

Living there made all the difference. Mom and I got along well, and in some ways we were closer than we had ever been. I spent a great deal of time in her apartment, but the fact that I had my own place to go back to changed our relationship. I was happy with the arrangement, and it made up a little for the fact that I was missing Aleksandr.

In May, I met Tony Fitzpatrick in Oliver's, a local restaurant I often went to with my friends on Wednesday nights. Tony was a real character, an ex-Houston Oiler with a heavy Texas drawl. He had the biggest appetite of anyone I've ever seen. We went out for dinner one night and he devoured four appetizers, two entrees, and three desserts. I was fascinated. He weighed 270 pounds and when we walked side by side, we must have looked like a hilarious couple.

A few weeks later we were walking down Rideau Street together. We weren't really dating, but we had become friends. All of a sudden, Bob came out of a store with another girl. The two of them were laughing together, and didn't see us at first. When he did catch sight of us, he stopped, confused. I felt jealousy welling up inside me. I was furious. I knew I had no right to be, but I couldn't help myself. He was icily polite to us, and passed on without introducing me to his companion, or waiting for an introduction to Tony.

That evening, the telephone rang, and it was Bob. He told me he had to see me.

"What for?" I asked coldly.

"I don't want to talk about it over the phone," he said.

In the end, I told him he could come over. He was there within half an hour.

"Elizabeth," he began, before he'd even got inside the door, "I have to tell you that when I saw you today with that guy, I wanted to punch him out. I was so jealous I didn't know what to do."

I stared at him. "*You* were jealous?" I said. "I was so jealous I couldn't see straight."

He came over to me and we hugged and kissed and said how much we had missed each other. We talked for a long time.

After a while he said, "Shall we try again?"

I didn't say anything for a moment. I wanted so much to try, but I knew it would be a mistake. In the end I shook my head. "Bob, it won't work. Something has gone from our relationship and we can't get it back. It isn't the same now. I think we should just leave things the way they are. If we try again, we'll just end up hating each other."

He knew I was right and he accepted what I said. I was glad that we had seen each other again and got things out into the open, and that we were parting on friendly terms this time, but it made me a little bit sad to see him go. He had been a big part of my growing up and becoming independent, and I will always be grateful to him for that.

Chapter Fifteen

I trained furiously all summer, concentrating hard on my figures and my jumps. We put a program together, using music from *Irma la Douce* and A Canadian Concerto and we choreographed it to suit my strengths. The program emphasized speed and continuous motion — I covered every square inch of the ice, flying from one element to another. Frances DaFoe, a Canadian skating judge who is also a well-known designer, offered to make a costume for me. At home, Mom and I continued to worry about money, searching in vain for a sponsor. But we were in the wrong city — Ottawa is not a skating stronghold like Toronto.

I didn't hear from Aleksandr, and I began to worry that something had happened to him. One day in early September, Mom and I went out for dinner in the evening, and when we were almost at the end of the meal, she reached into her purse and pulled out a big white envelope. She handed it to me and said, "By the way — I forgot. There's a letter from Aleksandr." I jumped, grabbed the letter, and tore it open eagerly. As I read it, I felt myself begin to shiver. He wrote to say that his wife was pregnant. They were expecting their first child in March. I felt depressed by the news, and I couldn't look at Mom for a while. I just sat there staring at the letter in my hands.

Later at home, I cried and told Mom what he had said. "Elizabeth, you wouldn't want him not to have children," she said. "He'll be a wonderful father." I knew that, and I did want him to be happy. But at the back of my mind I had always kept alive the hope that one day we might end up together. Now I knew it would never happen.

Skate Canada was held in Calgary in the fall, and something very peculiar happened. They had chosen Calgary to give the city a chance to prepare for the 1988 Olympics by hosting an international event. It also gave the skaters a chance to get used to the Saddledome. I noticed immediately that the ice was very hard. Skaters need fairly soft ice so the edges of the blade can bite the ice — this helps especially in taking off for jumps. The Saddledome was mostly used for hockey and hockey players prefer hard ice, because they need to glide over it using the middle of the skate blade. But I had trained in so many different arenas with so many different kinds of ice I was used to difficult conditions. Still, I pitied the skaters from places like Colorado, where they always train on a special figure-skating rink under ideal conditions. Those skaters would have problems adjusting.

However, what I didn't notice at first was that both ends of the Saddledome are identical. There is no way to distinguish one end from another. You couldn't tell where you were in the arena. Once the competitor was on the ice, they closed the entrances, and there were four television cameras in the four corners.

My first element was a spin, and when I came out of it, I went the wrong way. I didn't twig to the problem until the very end of my program, when I entered the combination jump. Everything felt weird, but I completed the program without mishap. When I got back to where Peter was standing, he had a very odd expression on his face. "Did you know that you just skated your whole program backwards?" he asked.

I won the silver medal at Skate Canada, but I didn't really feel I deserved it. I hadn't been at my best and I knew it. I'd felt rattled and overexcited. After a while, I came to a painful conclusion. I realized that Sonya was throwing me off. I adored Sonya, and at home her infectious enthusiasm was inspiring. I thrived on it. But to be around her during competitions had the opposite effect. It was overstimulating and I couldn't settle down. I asked her if she would stay away until after I'd skated my programs in future, and only join me when the marks were being announced. I hoped she would understand why I had to make such a request. The upcoming Olympics were too important for us to take any chances. I had to do everything right this time.

❄

During my preparations, I got a call from an official of the Canadian Mental Health Association. He had heard about what happened to me in Lake Placid, and about how I had made a comeback from depression. He asked me if I would like to act as a spokesperson on their behalf. I was very pleased to do this; I felt it was important for people to understand what I had gone through and also to know that when such things happen, it is not the end of the world. It is possible to fight back against mental illness, and I was happy to tell people what I had gone through and how I had recovered.

From that point on, I tried to mention the Canadian Mental Health Association when I was doing any public speaking, and they thanked me in a unique and delightful way. Every time I competed or performed, they sent flowers — daisies, the emblem of their association. They still do, and it always gives me a lift to see those bright yellow and white flowers in some unfamiliar dressing room or hotel room.

Charlene Wong and I spent a lot of time together, because she was also training with Peter and Sonya in Ottawa. I enjoyed her company, she was full of life and fun, even though she was having a few health problems.

The Canadian championships were held in Victoria, British Columbia, that January. Victoria is a beautiful city, reached by a boat ride from Vancouver through small, wooded islands in the Strait of Juan de Fuca. We stayed at the Empress, a big, old Canadian Pacific hotel, where every afternoon they serve tea in the lobby with cucumber sandwiches and tiny squares of fruit cake.

I ran into David Dore just before the Ladies event began. I wanted very much for him to say something encouraging to me. But he just nodded and passed by. Sometimes I felt like an outsider where the association was concerned, and it bothered me.

I won the gold medal in Victoria, and Charlene won the silver. We became very excited when we realized we were now both on the Olympic team.

Some members of the press were lukewarm toward me, in spite of the fact that I had retained my title. They were expecting Brian Orser to get an Olympic medal, and naturally touted Katarina Witt for the Ladies event, with Debi Thomas in second place and Caryn Kadavy in third.

When I got back to Ottawa, the *Ottawa Citizen* sent a photographer to take a picture of me with my puppy Pixie. I was glad that they seemed to be supporting me — or so I thought. But the next day the photo was published beside a headline that read "Manley Dogged by Inconsistency."

A few days later, David Dore called my club and asked to speak to me. He wanted to work with me, and also to clear the air between us. At that time, we were doing competitive simulations at the Ottawa Civic Centre, which involved rehearsing our programs under conditions as similar as possible to the actual Olympics. People would sit in the stands to act as audience and others would act as judges, announcers, and so forth. Peter Jensen arranged these simulations to get us used to the psychological stress of competing.

David Dore came to the Civic Centre and we worked together on the ice for two hours. He made a number of helpful suggestions, including one for the entrance into my triple lutz that really improved my ability to land the jump consistently. We also talked about my relationship with the association and why I had always felt that I didn't fit in. He was sympathetic, but he reminded me that criticism is part and parcel of the life of a top competitor, and that I shouldn't take things too personally. The association wanted me to keep getting better and better, and that meant correcting me when I did something wrong. We parted on good terms, and at last I felt that he was really behind me.

Just as I was beginning to feel more accepted and confident, however, someone called Peter Dunfield and told him that I had been seen hanging around in a bar late at night. He was furious with me. I was extremely upset when he didn't seem to believe me when I told him that nothing could have been further from the truth. I was going home every night after practice and flopping in front of Mom's television. I even ate sitting there. I hadn't the energy to go out — it would have been far too exhausting to bother putting on makeup and dressing up. I couldn't think of anything but the coming competitions.

Peter, however, didn't appear to accept my version of things. At the rink one morning he complained that I looked overtired.

"You're just not cutting it, Elizabeth," he said. "You must have been out late again last night."

"I was in bed by eleven," I told him heatedly.

He just looked at me and shook his head. "Is that right? It's not what I heard."

No matter what I said, he wouldn't listen. I even asked Sonya to talk to him for me.

"After four years, how can he not trust me?" I asked her. "It's weird."

The rumors continued. I couldn't understand why people were saying these things. I was leading a remarkably quiet life. Even to put on my coat and go out to a movie was a major effort. I tried to ignore the stories, but they disturbed me. I didn't know where they came from or why they didn't stop.

Now that we were so close to the Olympics, I concentrated on planning my strategy. I had learned a hard lesson at the last Olympics, having lost ground by too much partying and socializing. This time around, I knew better. I talked it over with Peter, and we decided that we would fly to Calgary for the opening ceremonies and then fly back to Ottawa until two days before the Ladies event began. That way, I would be removed from the worst temptations in the Olympic Village. I would also have more ice time to practice my programs up to the last minute, which had also been a problem in Sarajevo. Charlene agreed to do the same thing, as did Peter's British student and Olympic entrant, Gina Fulton, who was training with us.

A few days before we were scheduled to leave, I came down with a flu bug. I had a high fever and a sore throat, and I went straight to bed after the afternoon practice and slept until the following morning. When I woke up, I felt even worse. Mom came down to my apartment and took my temperature. It was 102.

I grew progressively worse over the next few days, and was unable to train properly. Peter told me that he felt I shouldn't fly out for the opening, but should wait in Ottawa and just go to my event. I thought it over, but in the end I decided to go. I wanted so much to be a part of those ceremonies — especially since the Games were being held in Canada. I was proud of being part of the home team.

The effort was worth it. Charlene, Gina, and I all caught the Olympic spirit and absorbed the atmosphere. We flew back the next morning to Ottawa and continued to train with total commitment and concentration. The three of us had made a pact — that we would all wear our team jackets while we were in Ottawa and try to retain the feeling of being part of the Games.

I spent some time that week talking to Charlene about the dangers of the Olympic Village. About being caught up in the excitement and the late nights and parties, and about meeting so many new people. She listened and promised to remember when the time came.

Even though we were at home, we still had Olympic fever. We watched each day's events on television, and enjoyed the celebrations, the interviews, and the commentaries. In a way it was tough for us, not being there and not being able to experience it at first hand, but in the end it proved to be a good decision.

My health deteriorated during the week we were back in Ottawa. Peter was in despair. He didn't know what to do with me. I had a double ear infection, and there wasn't much anyone could do for it. The drug testing rules for the Games prevented me from taking anything for it. My throat felt raw and my head ached. I wasn't sure I could make it, but I refused to give in. I had to give it a try.

The day before we left, I couldn't even get through my long program. I couldn't breathe properly. My breath came in long, rasping gasps, and I fought to keep my focus. Both Peter and I knew it was going to be touch and go as to whether I would be able to compete at all, but neither one of us was willing to say so out loud.

I had been experiencing great difficulty visualizing my Olympic programs. I'm not sure why that was, but I had been trying every night for hours to think through each program perfectly. No matter how hard I tried, I couldn't seem to get through them. It seemed that the visualizing was following my physical difficulties closely.

I discussed this with Peter Jensen and told him how worried I was. I had been using the technique for a long time and I knew it was essential to the success of my performance. I had never forgotten what had happened at Geneva and hoped that I could manage a perfect visualization of my Olympic programs before I left for Calgary. He told me that I was under a lot of stress because of the flu, and that perhaps I was getting too obsessed with it, and that was blocking the flow of my imagination.

The night before we left for Calgary, I went to bed early. I felt terrible, my ears were blocked, my head was pounding. In the middle of the night, I suddenly woke up with a start and realized I had just visualized the perfect program. I immediately called Mom and woke her up to tell her.

"I just got it. I saw the whole program," I said excitedly.

"I'm so happy for you," she murmured sleepily. In the morning she must have wondered if she'd dreamed about the call.

❅

The plane journey has to be among my all-time worst experiences. Because we had changed our reservations, we couldn't get a direct flight. They had all been booked for months. We were forced to fly from Ottawa to Toronto, Toronto to Thunder Bay, Thunder Bay to Saskatoon, and Saskatoon to Calgary. With so many take-offs and landings, I was in agony. It felt as though my eardrums were about to burst, and the pain was excruciating. The flight attendants poured warm oil into my ears, stuffed them with cotton wool, and gave me cups to hold over them, all to no avail. I clung to Peter's arm, tears pouring down my face, trying hard not to scream.

I was so sick by the time I reached Calgary that I could hardly stand up. I sat rocking myself back and forth in the seat. When all the other passengers had gone, Peter helped me up and we made it to the door of the plane. I was dizzy and nauseated and I could barely walk. My head felt as if it were about to explode and every muscle ached unbearably.

As we came into the terminal, the Olympic mascots, Hidey and Howdy, came running to greet us. I recoiled — I couldn't even smile at them, I felt so awful. They had come to the airport to greet us, because we were late arriving and two of us were from the Canadian team. They tried to make us laugh, but I was too sick even to pretend. I said to them, "Sorry, guys, you just aren't doing it for me." It was sad, because they were trying to cheer me up.

We got to the hotel van, and Peter and the driver managed to get me inside. I curled up on the back seat, scrunched into the fetal position, trying to ease the stomach cramps.

Peter got me through registration at the Village without too much fuss, and Charlene and I made our way to our room in the Canadian building. She unpacked while I lay on the bed. Peter sent for the Olympic doctors, and when they came they told me I had severe ear infections, a high fever, and strep throat. But they also said there was very little they could do for me within the Olympic drug-testing regulations. In the end they gave me huge doses of Robitussin to stop my cough. That knocked me out for the entire night. When I woke up the next morning, the pain had subsided a little.

We were staying in the University of Calgary student residences, and they were typical college buildings. All the guys were in one end and all the girls in the other. In the middle were common rooms with televisions and coffee-making equipment. Each bedroom had two beds, two desks, and two closets. It was rather plain, but clean and comfortable.

I went down to practice early, stopping on the way for a cup of tea and some cereal. It was the first thing I had eaten for almost twenty-four hours. I laced up my skates and went out to do my first patch. Before I had been tracing for ten minutes I realized that my balance was way off. I was scared — I knew it had to be because of the ear infection, and I could see no way it was going to improve before we started to compete. I began to cry, leaning against Peter, feeling wretched and frustrated.

Peter persuaded me to get out on the ice again, to keep working no matter what. He stood, watching me closely, and then he called me over again. "Elizabeth," he said, "let me have a look at your blades."

He picked up my feet, one at a time, and examined the blades. Then he shook his head and sighed heavily. "I thought so. One of the settings is out of whack.

That's what's throwing you off balance." It wasn't the ear infection at all.

"What are we going to do?" I asked.

"Not much we can do right now," he replied. "It's far too late for any equipment changes. We'll just have to adjust to it."

I couldn't believe it — first the flu, now my blades were wrong. I seemed to be jinxed. With only one patch to practice a day, we had to work fast, but once I knew it wasn't my ears, I managed to adapt to the problem quickly. In spite of the flawed blade setting, I was doing quite well.

The only thing I couldn't do was complete run-throughs of my programs. I couldn't breathe well enough yet. I would get a hacking cough if I overexerted myself, and I was still very weak. But I continued to practice, and little by little things started to come together.

I stuck to the doctor's orders and went straight from my room to practice and back to the room again to rest. I slept all the time I wasn't on the ice and only went out to get something to eat.

A lot of the athletes from Sarajevo were surprised by my hermit-like existence. A couple of the ski jumpers and bobsledders I had been friendly with made remarks about the change in me. They couldn't understand it. One of the jumpers asked, "What happened to our party girl?"

It was fun rooming with Charlene because everything was new to her, and I could see myself in 1984 in Sarajevo as she enjoyed all the new experiences. The pairs skaters and the dancers had all finished competing, but

Charlene managed to keep her focus and not join in all their celebrations. It wasn't that she wouldn't have loved to party — I could see the pent-up excitement simmering inside her. But she kept it in control, practiced hard, and went to bed early.

I caught sight of Aleksandr only once, and he did his usual little wave to me. But we didn't try to get together. Mom arrived and settled in with a host family, and Dad and Betty were likewise settled with theirs.

I was deluged with telegrams and good-luck cards. I couldn't believe it. The press might be lukewarm, but the public wanted me to win. I read all the messages and felt that I had to represent all these people in my performance. It was a good feeling.

I also received a long box filled with beautiful yellow roses. I didn't even have to open the card to know who they were from — all through my years of training with Bob McAvoy, he had always sent me yellow roses before a competition, because he knew they were my favorite flower. I opened the little card attached to the ribbon and read "Good luck, Elizabeth. I know you can do it. Bob." It made me cry, the way he had chosen this moment to let me know that he still believed in me.

There were press conferences set up for all the major competitors, and I had one arranged for the night before the compulsory figures competition. I knew that Katarina Witt and Debi Thomas had each held one the previous day, at which several hundred members of the press had been present, as well as many radio and television reporters. For weeks the media had been building up what they dubbed "The Battle of the Carmens" between the two of them, because each had chosen to perform to music from Bizet's opera. Both had consulted ballet stars and this also generated a certain amount of media hype. (Caryn Kadavy, who had been widely touted as a possible bronze medalist, had had to withdraw because of illness.)

When I walked through the door into my own conference, I saw only a small handful of Canadian reporters. I was just not one of the skaters who interested the press at that moment. They had me pegged as a loser.

As we were leaving the room, Peter turned to me.

"You're upset, aren't you?" he asked.

"Of course I am," I said.

"Do you want to see this room filled for one of your conferences?" he asked.

I shook my head. "It's never going to happen."

He stopped me before I could go on. "It could happen," he said. "But you have to make it happen. All you have to do is win a medal."

When the figures started I was unusually nervous, because of the problems with my skate blade. I wasn't sure I'd had enough time to adjust to the change in balance. To make matters worse, I had to do the figures I found the most difficult even at the best of times, starting on my weaker foot — the left.

"Oh, Peter," I groaned, "why can't anything ever go right?"

I felt my legs shaking as I took up my axis and started to trace the first figure. By the time I had completed the final figure, the loop, I was feeling extremely insecure. I ran from the ice into the dressing room and burst into tears.

Peter came in to console me, but I was too upset. I was

convinced I would be at the bottom of the first ten, maybe eighth at best. That was too low to get me up into the medals against the competition I was facing. Suddenly a lady came in, looking around.

"Miss Manley?" she said. "You're supposed to report for drug testing."

"Why me?" I asked. "I didn't place. You must have made a mistake."

She shook her head. "No, Miss Manley. You were fourth. You'd better get down there right away."

My heart soared when I realized what this meant. I had been convinced that it was all over — that I was too far down to have any chance at all. And now here I was, still a contender. I started to cry all over again, and Peter and I hugged each other.

"Peter, you have to pinch me to make sure I'm not dreaming," I said.

Chapter Sixteen

I went back to the residence that night and got a really good night's sleep. I wasn't completely well yet, but the contrast with the way I had been feeling earlier made me euphoric. I kept very quiet, and the next morning I went to practice, ate a good breakfast, and went back to the room to rest. The short programs were to be in the afternoon, and Peter advised me not to go to the building too early. He arranged to call for me when it was time to go over. That way I wouldn't get uptight being around the other skaters too long.

I drove to the Saddledome in one of the courtesy buses. As I went in, I peeked into the rink for moment and was awed to see that there was not an empty seat in the house. At least 22,000 people were packed into those rows, and the air almost crackled with electricity. I knew that Mom and Dad were out there somewhere, but I tried not to think about it. It was overwhelming in a way I can't even begin to explain.

Back in the dressing room, I prepared carefully, putting on makeup, dressing slowly, stretching. Outside in the corridor, Peter Dunfield and Peter Jensen walked me through my program. I still hadn't gotten through it on the ice, so to some extent I would be flying blind in the competition. Then I went back into the dressing room and found a spot by myself, sat down to concentrate on a mental run-through, and managed to do it perfectly in my mind. By the time all this was finished, it was time to go out for warm-up.

I was uncharacteristically nervous during warm-up. I worried that I might start coughing, or that I wouldn't be able to breathe. I kept going over to the boards and Peter told me to calm down.

"Just relax, Elizabeth," he said. "Try to forget about your health. Just concentrate on the program. It'll come."

After the warm-up I had a chance to rest before it was my turn to skate. I was so nervous my teeth were chattering. But when my name was called and I moved to center ice to take up my position, something strange happened. For the first time in my entire career, I lost every shred of nervousness. I felt calm and confident and completely at home. My knees were steady, my breath was coming smoothly and evenly, I was actually enjoying myself.

I skated a near-perfect short program, the best I have ever skated. I landed every single one of the required elements, and I landed them cleanly. When it ended, I couldn't grasp what had just happened. I just stood there in the middle of the ice and grabbed my hair and thanked God. It was a terrific feeling, such a rush. I had gone through all that sickness and fear and had worried that I wouldn't make it through, and now here were twenty-two thousand people on their feet, cheering at the top of their lungs.

When I got off the ice, Peter and Sonya were there to hug me, but we knew we couldn't get excited yet, because this was just the short program, and it counted for only 30 percent of the overall score. I had come third in the short program (after Katarina and Debi), and that moved me up to third place overall. Debi was in first place and Katarina was second. I knew that if I could only hang on, I might be able to win a medal.

We had a day off between the short and the long programs, which was probably the best thing that could have happened. It gave me an opportunity to come down to earth again, to calm myself before the final round. I practiced in the early morning, but I still couldn't get through my entire four-minute routine. That made me a little nervous again. But I did get through all the triples and spins. The entire Canadian hockey team came into the arena while I was practicing and they wished me luck. It meant a lot to me that they took the trouble to come and cheer me on.

I went to bed early and slept well that night, waking only once when Charlene came in. I muttered something and promptly fell asleep again. Peter came for me the next morning, and we had a light breakfast of boiled eggs and toast. Then I went back to the Saddledome and had a really good practice. We didn't push it, we just went through the elements until we got them right, and then I stopped.

I spent the rest of the morning with Peter Jensen. He talked to me about the competition, but not in a way that made me nervous. He helped me to relax and prepare. I felt great by the time I left him, and went back to my room to rest.

In the late afternoon, Peter Dunfield came by and took me out for a good meal. "Let's treat ourselves," he said. "Let's order something extravagant." I chose a small sirloin steak, because that's my favorite, and Peter had grilled scampi. I ate slowly, making sure I wouldn't get indigestion. Then we went back to the Village. Peter told me that he and Peter Jensen would be going over to the Saddledome to be with Charlene, who was in the early stages of the competition. They would phone me when it was time for me to come over, and one of the team leaders would drive me there in a van.

I have always had a superstition about being perfectly clean and organized. I can't bear even the slightest thing to be out of place, and at competitions I have always had all my stuff packed ready to leave before I skate the long program. My laundry would be all done, everything in my room neat and tidy as though I'd never been there. It was something I felt compelled to do, and just because this was the Olympics I didn't see any reason to change my habits. I started to do my washing, and I was still folding the clean laundry when the Ladies final had started over at the rink. I sat in the common room, folding T-shirts and sweatpants, calmly watching the coverage on television.

Several of the ski jumpers and bobsledders I had met in Sarajevo were there, watching the television too. At first they just said "Hi" and sat there, and then I saw this funny look come over their faces as they looked at the television screen, then at me, then back at the screen. Finally one of them said, "Liz. aren't you supposed to be over there competing? What happened — did you pull out?"

I couldn't help laughing at their confusion, because it must have looked strange, me standing there folding my laundry during my own competition. I explained that I still had plenty of time, and they all wished me luck.

As it turned out, the timing was just right. I got to the Saddledome half an hour before the actual warm-up. I went into the dressing room, pulled on my tracksuit, and started walking around. I saw a group of television cameramen following Debi and Katarina, and I was amused when one of them tried to follow Katarina into the ladies room. He was looking through his viewfinder and didn't notice where he was going.

I did my visualization with Peter Jensen, then I went over to the far side of the arena, away from everyone, and sat there by myself, trying to keep calm. I stayed there until it was time to go back for the warm-up.

I had a shaky warm-up. It made Peter very nervous, because I fell on things I'd been getting right all week. I missed a couple of triple lutzes, which had gone perfectly during practice. When I got off the ice, I could see both Peters were uptight, but I was actually feeling just fine.

Katarina skated right before me. As she came off the ice, I could tell she wasn't completely satisfied from the expression on her face. The applause was quite good, but I couldn't help noticing that her coach didn't come forward to embrace her as she always did when Katarina had done well. I tried not to think about it, though, so I wouldn't lose my own focus.

My name was called, and I flew out to center ice and waited for my music to start. Suddenly I saw the crowd stand up with a great roar. Everyone started to applaud wildly, whistling and cheering loudly. I thought the roof might fall in, the noise was so thunderous. I didn't know what to do, so I skated back to the side, waving. Peter told me to take some deep breaths and wait for it to subside.

"Try to block them out," he warned. "Don't let them throw you."

Eventually a hush fell over the arena and I went back out and took up my position. When the music started, I felt as though I were riding on the wings of the crowd's ovation. I was inspired — I felt wonderful. I approached the triple lutz without hesitation, and when I hit it right, I let out a yell of delight. Immediately I landed, I forced myself to focus again, shutting everything else out, seeing only the ice ahead of me and the shimmer of the boards as they spun past. I was possessed. Any worries I'd had about getting through the program vanished. I was on such a high, I felt I was actually flying, and I didn't miss a single thing. When I slid to a stop, I was in shock. I started to cry, relieved, happy, and overwhelmed all at once.

Everyone in the audience seemed to be screaming. I looked for Mom, she was the first person I thought of. I wanted so much to see her, and I called her name out loud. We had gone through so much to reach this point, and now I wanted to share this moment with her. I was so intent on trying to spot her that I forgot to bow.

Suddenly a huge white cowboy hat came sliding across the ice toward me. I leaned over and scooped it up and jammed it on my head. I gave the crowd a thumbs-up sign and they went wild all over again. The ice was covered in flowers, but I didn't wait to pick them up. I wanted to get off so I could be with Peter and Sonya and Peter Jensen, the three people who had worked so hard to bring me to this moment. I wanted to hug them all and tell them how much they meant to me. When I got to them, I saw that Peter had tears running down his face, and I knew I must have done something very special, because Peter never cries.

I will never forget those moments as long as I live. They were the most exciting moments of my life. A medal didn't even matter, it suddenly became unimportant. After all we had gone through in the preceding weeks, not being able to get through the programs, the blade problems, the figures, the pain, the indifference of the press, the rumors and misunderstandings with Peter, and all the years of struggle and hardship, I had done the performance of my life and the crowd knew I had won. It was an incredible feeling.

Then the technical marks came up: 5.9, 5.7, 5.8, 5.9, 5.9, 5.9, 5.7, 5.8, 5.9. I felt terrific, remembering something Toller had told me before I left Victoria: "Skating well is the best revenge." I now knew exactly what he meant, because I am sure that nobody had expected me to do well at the 1988 Olympic Games, it even seemed at times that nobody *wanted* me to do well, and I had, in fact, had my revenge.

The second set of marks (for artistic interpretation) came up: 5.8, 5.8, 5.9, 5.8, 5.7, 5.8, 5.8, 5.9, 5.8. I ran over to the CTV commentators' area, where Johnny Esaw, Debbie Wilkes, and Brian Pockar were standing. Brian was crying, he was so happy. I hugged him, because he had always been a staunch supporter of mine, and at times like this, you remember that sort of thing.

Then I realized that there were still a couple more skaters to perform, and I told Peter I wanted to go and watch Debi Thomas. I had a hard time getting through, everyone had come running down the stairs to congratulate me, and all the Canadian team members were kissing me and slapping me on the back and Charlene was trying to fix my hair where the cowboy hat had flattened it.

I watched Debi, and she was really not at her best. She was clearly nervous, and probably the crowd's reaction to my performance had made her lose her concentration. When I heard her marks, I knew that I had won a medal. I hadn't let myself think about it up till then, but now I knew I had done it.

I ran to Peter and Sonya, and the computer placement came up. I had won the silver, and had come within a fraction of a point of beating Katarina. Debi was third. Most exciting of all, I had won the gold medal for free skating. I burst into tears all over again. In the middle of all this, someone came racing down the stairs to tell me that the Prime Minister was on the phone for me.

Prime Minister Mulroney told me that he had watched the competition with his children, whom I knew from several functions we had attended together in Ottawa. He said that he was proud that I came from the National Capital Region and even prouder that I was representing his country. He said his children were so excited that he couldn't get them to go to bed. I was touched that he had taken the trouble to call and congratulate me.

A few minutes later, I did a live television interview on CTV. During the interview, the Minister for Fitness and Amateur Sport, Otto Jelinek, came running up to me and gave me a big hug. He was clearly thrilled by my success. I was happy to have him there. Like any young skater in Canada, I was grateful to him for all he had done for the sport, especially during his own years as a world champion pairs skater.

Later the press said the usual things about politicians getting political mileage out of the Olympics, and they accused Otto of pulling a publicity stunt. That seemed unfair to me, after all Otto had done for sports in Canada. He had every right in the world to share that moment with me.

There was a press conference later on in the evening. I was the first person to arrive in the press room after the drug testing was over. Peter was right — this time the place was filled to the rafters, with press members from all over the world. I looked at Peter and he winked at me.

None of the reporters seemed to know anything about me. They weren't prepared. They had already written stories about Katarina and Debi, but nothing on me. Now they had to throw out all their stuff on "the Battle of the Carmens" and find a new hook, because some little half-pint nobody from Canada had snuck into the middle and changed the whole situation. I must admit, I enjoyed the feeling.

Chapter Seventeen

For the next few hours I was in the press room almost continuously. I took a brief period out for some rest and something to eat, but neither was appealing to me at that point. I wanted to keep right on talking. I gave interview after interview, and I turned no one down. I had so much to say, and it all came pouring out of me as if a dam had broken.

I saw Mom and Dad only briefly. I had waited for them at the arena and we had cried as we hugged each other, all three of us united for the first time in many years. It was wonderful to be able to share the victory with Mom, who had worked so hard for this moment and never once lost hope. And it was also a great feeling that I had finally proved to Dad what it had all been about. I felt, at last, that he was really proud of me.

I hadn't seen Aleksandr at all before the competition. I had avoided him, because he was the one person who might have thrown me off. But now he was waiting for me by the dressing rooms, and for the first time we threw away our caution and hugged and kissed right in the corridor. "I am so happy for you, my little Antoushka," he whispered. Just then his coach appeared and he had to let me go, but we both knew that we'd be on the tour following the Worlds and that we would have time to see each other then.

Charlene waited until most of the other people had gone before she came to see me. She hugged me so hard that I gasped, and told me how thrilled she was. I told her that she only had to wait four more years and then I would be the one congratulating her. Back in our room that night we talked until we were worn out, and then she fell into an exhausted sleep.

I couldn't sleep at all. I lay awake, staring into the darkness, and suddenly I knew what I wanted to do more than anything. I crept out of bed and into the corridor outside where the telephones were, and I dialed Bob McIsaac's number. I waited impatiently as it rang, and then he answered, obviously wide awake. "I knew you were going to call," he said. "I'm so happy for you." We talked for half an hour, and all the old warmth was there between us. I guess it always will be.

The next morning, early, Peter Jensen came to collect me so that we could get some breakfast before we went to practice for the exhibitions. The buildings are connected to a central cafeteria by tunnels, which at this hour were deserted and dark. As Peter and I were walking, we approached two elderly janitors, busily mopping the floor of the tunnel. When we drew level with them, they looked up. Without a word, they dropped their mops, stood to attention, and began to applaud. It was so unexpected, so spontaneous, that it sent chills right through me. I was very moved. Peter said that in all his years of working with world-class athletes, he had never experienced anything like it before.

That day I was applauded by people everywhere I went. Total strangers would start to clap as I passed, and many of them called out to me. I seemed to have touched a chord in them; it was a nice feeling. They saw me as one of their own, and I hadn't really understood it until then. It was all happening so fast. In the press room, some of the reporters had told me how I had given the whole country a boost and lifted its spirits, but I hadn't felt it before. Now I knew it was true, and I was very proud.

At the exhibitions I skated to "Sing a Song" by Barbara Cook. It was the perfect choice, since I felt like singing myself. I could feel the enthusiasm and support of the audience and I reveled in every second.

After the exhibitions were over, I sat on the plane back to Ottawa, reeling from a mixture of exhaustion and euphoria. I slept most of the way back, slumped between Sonya and Peter, and only woke up to sign autographs for the crew.

The lobby of the Ottawa airport building had one entire glass wall, and as the plane came to a halt, I could see thousands of people waiting inside the lobby, milling around behind the windows. I had no idea what this was all about, and I heard Peter chuckle to himself. He turned to me with a big smile on his face. "Well, Elizabeth, I told you what you had to do, didn't I? Just win a medal. Now you see what I meant."

The flight attendant came back as the passengers

were about to disembark and asked Charlene and me to remain behind until all the other passengers had gone. Then some RCMP officers boarded, saluted us, and escorted us off through all those wildly cheering people. It was like being royalty. I couldn't quite take it all in. We were taken into the VIP lounge inside the terminal, and my whole family was there. We hugged and cried and laughed and my brothers told me how proud they were. Mom and I looked at each other for a long moment, with tears running down our faces.

"Mom," I said. "Can you believe it? After all those years? All that hard work? All the sacrifices you made?"

"I never doubted it for a minute, Elizabeth," she said. "Never for one single minute."

Dad was beaming, and I went over and took his arm and looked up at him. "I had to do this, Dad," I said. "I wanted so much for you to understand why it was so important to me. I needed you to realize why I didn't go to college and I wanted you to be proud of me."

Dad hugged me and ruffled my hair, the way he used to do when I was little. "I'm proud of you, all right," he said. "But what you don't seem to understand is that I've *always* been proud of you."

When we came out of the lounge, the RCMP warned me that there was a large crowd waiting downstairs. They said that five thousand people had come to the airport to greet me, the largest crowd since our CFL team had won the Grey Cup twenty years before. They had had to close down the airport. Some people had been waiting there all night.

As I came down the escalator, a deafening roar went up, and I saw people with balloons and banners reading

"We love you, Elizabeth." People were holding out bouquets of flowers and others were waving Canadian flags. I was amazed.

Outside, there was a stretch limousine waiting for us, sent by the City of Gloucester. I rode along the familiar route, seated between Mom and Dad, and felt wonderful. I held their hands for most of the ride home.

When I got home and walked into my apartment, there were so many sacks of mail, I could hardly move. I didn't know where to begin. Hundreds of people had also sent flowers, but Mom arranged to have these sent on to hospitals, along with most of the gifts, but she had kept a record of who had sent what, so that I could write and thank the people who had sent them.

That night I stayed up for hours, reading the notes, letters, and telegrams. As I read, I kept thinking how strange it was that I had touched the lives of all these people I had never met and would probably never meet — that an event like the Olympics could mean so much to them and inspire them, affecting their own lives. I made a vow then and there that I would reply to each one personally. I read until I could no longer see, then I crawled into bed and fell asleep.

Over the next few days, more letters poured in, until they totalled several thousand. Answering them took me months, but I did manage to reply to them all in the end. I did a few every time I had a free evening until they were all finished.

❄

A few months before, I had contacted a manager, Michael Rosenberg, and asked him if he would consider representing me when I retired from amateur skating. I had originally been nervous about meeting such a well-known "Hollywood agent," who had managed such skating stars as Barbara Underhill and Paul Martini, Tai Babilonia, and Randy Gardner, but when I met him, he put me completely at ease. Now he flew to Ottawa and we discussed my next move.

Michael is a tall man with blond hair, blue eyes, and a brilliant smile. Tired as I was, his energy and enthusiasm infected me, as we talked about Calgary. The first decision we had to make was whether or not I should continue on to the Worlds. Now that I had won a silver medal in the Olympics, I had an offer from the Ice Capades. A medal at the Worlds wouldn't improve the offer, but a loss might harm it. I had to weigh up the pros and cons very carefully. On the one hand, if I went on to the Worlds and won another medal, I would prove once and for all that my Olympic win wasn't just a fluke. On the other hand, if I competed and lost, I would diminish my Olympic placement and possibly damage my professional prospects. The latter was not something to be taken lightly, because Mom and I at this point had barely a penny to our names.

Michael said he thought I should go, but he added that he would support me whatever decision I took. I asked my family and the Dunfields and fellow skaters and people at the Canadian Figure Skating Association, and got a variety of different opinions. Some people thought I should get out while the going was good and others said I'd be nuts to quit now. The association wanted me to continue and win them a medal, but Mom and Peter, whose opinions I valued most, said I had to make up my own mind. "You're the one who has to live with it," Mom said. "It's up to you."

We were only two weeks away from the start of the Worlds in Budapest, and I couldn't come to a decision. I had a hard time concentrating on my training, because at this point my heart really wasn't in it. I went through the motions, but there was no fire in what I did. I was torn in two different directions.

Finally, a week before we were due to leave for Budapest, I sat down with Peter and told him that I had made up my mind to go on. "I have to do it," I explained. "I really don't have a choice. If I don't at least try, everyone will think of me as a flash in the pan at Calgary. They will think that winning the silver was a once-in-a-lifetime accident, not something that was the result of years of hard work and effort. I want to prove that I can do it again." I paused and looked at him. "Most of all, I need to prove it to myself, because if I don't try I will spend the rest of my life wondering if I could have done it."

Peter leaned forward and took me by the shoulders. "I knew you would come to this decision in the end," he said. "You aren't the sort of person who can quit when there's still a battle to be fought." He stood up and held out his hand. "Come on," he said, pulling me to my feet. "There's work to be done."

Over the next week I got back my fighting spirit. By the time we left for Budapest, I was prepared and ready to take them all on. Suddenly, this was the event I was really eager to get to. I still had some unfinished business to take care of.

The Worlds which follow the Olympics are always

difficult for skaters. There is so little time between the two events that it's hard to work up the energy again and to refocus after the excitement of the Games. Physically it is something of a downer, and it requires a monumental strength of will to regain the competitive drive to perform at top level. But when I arrived in Hungary, my energy was returning and my motivation was as high as ever. I was ready for a fight — and I knew there probably would be a fight in store for me.

Chapter Eighteen

I was now one of the favorites of the press instead of the forgotten competitor. Everyone wanted to interview me, and Peter became anxious that I would overtire myself before I got out on the ice to compete. People wrote stories calling me things like "the Rocky of skating" and "the little kid from Canada who could topple the Queen." It put a certain amount of pressure on me, but it also fueled me. I had waited a long time to be taken seriously, and I thrived on the attention. It was hard to believe that it was only three weeks since the press had written me off as an also-ran.

When I went to skate the compulsory figures, I was feeling as confident as I ever had in my life. I was completely prepared, mentally and physically, and I was actually smiling to myself as I waited to skate my first figure. I traced sure and well-shaped circles on the ice, and won the first and second figures. I was enjoying

myself — I had finally mastered the difficult art of figures, and I sat happily beside Peter, waiting to be called
for the third figure.

Suddenly I saw Peter's face change. He frowned, then
he let out a whistle of disbelief. "I don't believe it!" he
almost shouted. I looked up at the scoreboard. The
combined standings after the first two figures had just
gone up. Katarina Witt was in first place, I was in second. We stared at the numbers in shock, unable to take
it in. Peter went over to the judges and demanded an
explanation, and was told it was because of the
ordinals. Mom, who had been watching and had taken
down all the scores, shook her head. "It just isn't possible," she said. "I've been keeping score and you ought
to be ahead by a wide margin."

We didn't know what to do. No one could understand
it. We considered launching an appeal, but knew that if
we did that, I might be penalized during the free skating, which is much harder to challenge. So we sat there,
helpless, knowing that I had won those two figures, and
powerless to do anything about the political structure of
the event. It seemed that there was some kind of unwrit-
ten taboo against dethroning a reigning Olympic champion.

"Elizabeth," Peter said at last, "I want you to try to
put it right out of your mind. Forget it. You have to
accept it, because there isn't anything we can do to
change it. I know it isn't fair, but that's the way it is in
skating and we just have to live with it."

I nodded and walked away, trying to refocus and
gather my energy again. I wasn't about to forget it. I was

furious, and I was planning to go out there and skate the best third figure the judges had ever seen in their lives.

Katarina skated three places before me. She missed the center of her loop twice, a major mistake that I felt would have to prove fatal in a World Championship. I looked carefully and there was no doubt about it. She had blown the figure. She had to be marked down. Peter even went out and photographed it, so as to have some kind of record.

Just before it was my turn to skate, Peter said to me, "Elizabeth, if you think you can skate an absolutely clean loop, then you should go and lay it out right beside Katarina's. But it has to be the best loop you've ever skated. If you're even the tiniest bit nervous or unsure, then you should take a patch of ice farther away."

I didn't hesitate. I knew I could do a better loop with my eyes shut. I was fired up, hopping mad, and I wanted to put my loop right next to Katarina's so everyone could see. I might not change the judges' minds, but I would at least feel better.

I went and laid out the best loop of my career, in or out of competition. It was as close to perfect as it could have been. The Canadian press were milling around, and some of them even went out and examined the two loops side by side. There was no doubt — I had to win, based on those loops. But when the marks were announced, they gave first place to Katarina, and second place to me. Peter just shook his head at me. There was nothing we could do.

I was now more determined than ever, fired up for the

short program. I had never felt better, and I went out to warm up full of energy. I threw off a whole row of triples that had the audience cheering. When I finally got off, my eyes must have been blazing, because Peter took me by the shoulders and told me to calm down. "You'll injure yourself if you aren't careful," he warned.

I felt completely focused as I stood on the ice waiting for my music to start, and I sailed through the first couple of elements with ease. Just as I was approaching the big combination jump, however, my music stopped. I faltered and slid to a standstill. The tape had broken. I was numb with disbelief. It had been years since anyone's tape had broken down at a World Championship.

I skated over to the boards, and the crowd groaned in sympathy. I fought back tears, and Peter put his arm around me. "Don't let it get to you," he said.

By the time the tape had been fixed, my concentration had been shattered. I was made to skate from the beginning, and I was no longer as sharp and focused as I had been the first time. I missed the vital combination jump and dropped to third place. I was devastated, and began to wonder if I would even be able to hold on to third place under these conditions.

We had a day off in between the short program and the long, and Peter and I spent the day practicing and discussing what was happening. Finally we decided that I just had to go out there and get it over with. It didn't really matter any more. We couldn't change the system. The important thing was to put it behind us and get on with our lives.

Even so, I was fighting mad when I went out to do my long program. I made a few errors, because one always does under such extreme pressure. But I held on to everything, even my triple lutz. I was leaning so far forward on the landing that I ought to have fallen, but I somehow defied gravity and hung on to it. It was a tiny miracle that I didn't go down. Slightly unnerved, I lost confidence just as I was approaching the triple toe loop, so I made it into a double instead. But part of my brain reminded me that I needed that extra triple to make up the technical difficulty in my program. All through the rest of my program I looked for a chance to fit it in, and shortly before the end I managed it. And I landed it cleanly. I finished the program with such energy that I could have skated for another five minutes.

As I spun to a stop, the audience started cheering. I was elated. I knew I had done well, almost as well as I had done at the Olympics. I wondered what the judges were going to do, and when I came off the ice, I could tell that Peter was thinking the same thing.

Katarina, although she had missed some of her elements and had doubled some of her triples, was given very good marks. As the marks came up, I saw that the judges had done the same thing as at the Olympics. I was awarded the silver medal and Katarina was the world champion. It was the most frustrating feeling imaginable. I was second in the figures, and I had won the combined free skating, but I was still in second place.

Later, when it was all over, I thought about it in a different light and began to feel better. In spite of coming second, I felt that I had actually improved on my Olympic achievement, closing the gap between Katarina and me to a very narrow slit, and proved, at least to my own satisfaction, that my Olympic silver medal was not a fluke.

I did, however, manage to give Katarina one surprise that night. As we were standing on the podium together, waiting for Debi to join us, I turned to her and said, "Did you know Debi just got married?" Katarina's jaw dropped. I told her that Debi had been married to a University of Colorado student about ten days before, but she hadn't told anyone; she wanted it to be a secret until after the Worlds.

I flew back to Ottawa right after the exhibition was over. I told Michael that I didn't want to do the European phase of the I.S.U. tour, as I needed a chance to rest before I did the American part of the tour. I was exhausted, not fully recovered from the flu bug that had felled me just before the Olympics. I had turned pro now and honestly felt I should opt out of the tour.

Michael arranged a compromise for me in the end. I was allowed to miss the first two weeks of the European tour, but then I had to fly over and complete it. Otherwise I would be banned from the North American tour, which I was very anxious to skate. Apart from anything else, Michael felt it was very important that I appear on that tour to reinforce my success in Calgary.

During the two weeks I was back in Ottawa, I signed a multi-year contract with the Ice Capades, the largest ever signed by a Canadian. Tom Scallen, the president of the Ice Capades, gave me a $50,000 cheque as a signing bonus. I knew exactly what I was going to do with it. As soon as the signing was over, I went straight to the bank and paid off Mom's debts, which by that time totalled $26,000. Mom's face when I told her was well worth it. I felt fantastic, being able to pay my own way at last.

I knew I had Michael to thank for that, and he managed to negotiate all sort of other deals for me — a television special, Elizabeth Manley skates by the Montreal firm of Daoust, even an Elizabeth Manley doll (made by an Ottawa firm). He had been hard at work behind the scenes, just waiting for the moment when I would turn professional. It was an exciting time, and I raced from appointment to appointment, doing even more press interviews and trying to wade through my stacks of fan mail.

Michael kept in touch all the way through the tour, and he told me all about the exciting opportunities he had come up with for me. He and his wife Nancy had taken over the roles of Peter and Sonya in my life, and I loved working with them. Nancy was always there with a word of encouragement and Michael, who was invariably kind and thoughtful to me, protected me like a mother tiger with one cub when it came to the rest of the world. Although he is always suave and charming, he is known as a brilliant businessman and a merciless negotiator.

❉

As I left for Europe again and the I.S.U. tour, Michael saw me off at the airport. I felt very secure, knowing that he was in my corner, and I knew that he was the right manager for me. As I was about to pass through security and go into the departure lounge, he held my arm and said, "This is the last thing you will ever have to do as an amateur. When this is over, you will be earning enough money to take care of yourself and your Mom for the rest of your life." I thought about what he had said on the plane on the way to London, considering what a difference my being professional would make to our lives.

In London I saw Aleksandr for the first time since we had hugged each other outside the dressing room in Calgary. I had avoided him in Budapest, feeling very strange about the impending birth of his first child, and not feeling quite right about being with him.

The two of us went to dinner in a little restaurant in Soho, far away from the prying eyes of the skating world. We talked about what was happening in our lives and how different things would be now that I was leaving the amateur circuit. Aleksandr was sad about it — I could see it in his eyes — and I knew that this was the last time we would be able to be together like this. At one point I leaned over and touched his face. "It's all right," I said. "I know this can't go on. You have a family to take care of and I have a career. . ."

"What about you, Antoushka?" Aleksandr asked. "Won't you find a nice man to marry and love?"

I sighed. "Perhaps. One day. If I meet the right man. But I shall always think of you with affection, no matter where I am. I shall always carry you in my heart."

He smiled. "I shall always have you in my heart also. I shall never forget you, Antoushka." He kissed my hand and held it for a long moment. "Promise me something?" he asked. "Promise me you will not spend your life alone. You must marry and have a family of your own."

I smiled at him. "I'm sure I will, Aleksandr. And I promise that when I do, you'll be the first to know."

＊

Back in North America, I was riding on a wave of euphoria. I loved every minute of the I.S.U. tour, enjoying my new-found celebrity, skating well, and generally having a blast. Tommy Collins, the tour organizer, is a wonderful man, down-to-earth but fun-loving, and I adored working with him. There was always something special going on.

I grew very close to Tommy during the tour, and told him all about Aleksandr and Bob and how I couldn't seem to find the right man for me. I used to cry on Tommy's shoulder about it; he was one of the rare people you could do that with. One day, when we were walking around backstage before one of the shows, he introduced me to Paul Hendrickson, who was the technical coordinator on the show. Paul is a handsome, blue-eyed man, and Tommy noticed that I took to him immediately. He didn't say anything about it at the time, but he must have filed it away for future reference.

When we reached Kansas, Tommy told me that Paul wanted to see more of me, and I was delighted. What I didn't know was that he also told Paul that I wanted to see more of him, and he was apparently pleased too. We both thought that the other one had initiated things. Tommy set up a meeting at a restaurant, and when we got there, there was a bottle of Dom Perignon on the table from him. We sat there for hours, drinking champagne, and getting to know each other. I have never hit it off so completely with anyone on my first meeting.

For the next two weeks, however, I didn't hear from Paul, and I worried about it constantly. Poor Tommy — he went through hell with me. He kept telling me how busy Paul was, and how demanding the tour was for him, and that I shouldn't be concerned about it. He reassured me over and over again that Paul liked me, but I thought Paul had already forgotten our evening together.

Chapter Nineteen

That summer I gave up my apartment, because with all the touring I was about to do, it didn't seem to be worth holding on to it. I moved back in with Mom, and this time we got along beautifully together. She respected both my individuality and my independence. I, in turn, knew that she had a great deal of good sense to offer me, and I no longer resented her for it. We made a great team.

During the summer, one exciting thing happened after another. The cities of Ottawa and Gloucester held a ceremony in which I received the keys to each city from the mayor. Later, Ottawa named a big park in the Hunt Club area of the city after me, and Orleans renamed its arena "The Elizabeth Manley International Skating Center." It still gives me a funny feeling when I see the sign.

The New Brunswick company of McCain asked me to

do a commercial for them, for a new product they were introducing called Mr. Juicy. The commercial was fun because I got to do it with a great bunch of little kids — they had to chase me around on skates. We spent a wonderful day taping it.

I was invited to speak at a mental institution in Provo, Utah — one of the Charter Canyon Hospital Group. First I talked to a group of young people. They seemed very tough and bitter, and I couldn't tell if they were taking in what I said. Later I gave a speech in their lecture theater to the staff and patients. I was asked to speak for twenty minutes, but I wound up talking for an hour and a half. There was so much I wanted to say — about not giving up hope and about conquering mental illness. Afterward, one of the nurses told me that the young people I had spoken to earlier had also come to my speech. "They never do that," she said. "It's the first time they've ever asked to come to a lecture." So perhaps I made some impression on them after all.

The Ice Capades were to open in Duluth, Minnesota, and I arrived in July ready for rehearsals. I liked the company enormously and I couldn't wait to skate all the wonderful numbers they had planned for me. I lived in a hotel near the rink, and after practice each day I would go back and relax, reading, watching television, or answering letters.

One evening I was lying on the floor reading a magazine, when someone knocked at my door. I jumped up to answer it, and in a split second, without even my realizing what had happened, I broke my foot. It was one of those awful freak accidents that occur for no reason except bad luck. I was appalled. How would I ever be ready for opening night?

I went to hospital and got X-rays done, then they encased my foot in plaster and put me on crutches. I would be off the ice for at least six weeks. I immediately telephoned Michael and told him what had happened. "Oh, Michael," I said, "when is this streak of bad luck going to end?"

Michael called Tom Scallen and told him he thought I should go back to Ottawa so I could have my foot properly treated and Mom could look after me while I was recuperating. Tom, however, wanted me to stay in Duluth. He felt I could get better treatment where I was and he wanted me to be available for interviews. Michael was worried about me, stuck in a hotel room in the middle of Minnesota with a broken foot, but he could see Tom's point of view.

I survived and gradually my foot healed. A week before the show was to open, I finally got on to the ice again. I was panicky, because I hadn't learned the choreography and we hadn't finished all the blocking. We worked frantically, throwing it all together, going over and over the routines. After five days I knew most of the steps and was beginning to feel a bit more confident.

I hadn't seen Paul since the end of the I.S.U. tour, but I heard from him that week. He told me he would be coming to opening night. I was delighted, but it also threw me into a tailspin — I was already a nervous wreck, worrying about the kind of performance I would give, knowing my whole family would be at the show. Now Paul was going to be there too. I was almost hysterical.

I went down to the bar two evenings before we were due to open, looking for some of the girls from the show whom I'd made friends with. As I stood there looking around the room, Tom Scallen's producer-director, Willy Bietak, came up and said, "How are you feeling?"

I smiled. It was nice of him to be concerned about me. "All right, considering," I said.

He looked a bit apprehensive. "Then you'll be okay to fly to New York tomorrow after rehearsal?"

I laughed. I thought he was joking and trying to get me to relax. "Sure, Willy," I said. "Maybe I could go via Los Angeles while I'm at it!"

Willy's expression told me this was no joke. "Elizabeth, I'm really sorry, but I'm afraid there's no choice. 'Good Morning, America' wants you on the show, but only if we can get you there for tomorrow morning."

I gasped. "But Willy, I open tomorrow *night!*"

"I know," he said kindly. "We'll have you back in plenty of time for that, I promise. After all, it's every bit as important to us that you have a good debut as it is to you."

I still felt panicky. "Why can't we do a feed?" I asked. "I could do it from a local studio."

He shook his head. "We already asked about that, but the network has made up its mind. They want you to do it in person from New York."

I suddenly exploded. "Willy, there *must* be some other way! What if the flying makes my foot swell again? What if there's fog and I can't get back? I'm under-rehearsed as it is, and I need every second of ice time I can get to prepare."

Willy was calm. He put his hands on my shoulders

and said, "You'll be fine. You're a trooper. It'll all work out — you'll see. We wouldn't ask you if it wasn't important to the show."

I left the bar, went back to my room, and telephoned Michael. I poured out the story and he listened quietly as I begged him to intervene. Finally he said, "I know how you feel. But the professional world is a tough one — a lot of people depend on the Ice Capades in order to make their living, and if it doesn't get enough publicity, people won't buy tickets and everyone on the show will be affected. Publicity is part of your job. You're being paid a lot of money because people know who you are. When the chance of a network appearance comes up, you have to do it, no matter how inconvenient it may be. It's as important as your performance on the ice."

I sighed. I knew he was right, but it didn't make things any easier.

"There's something else," Michael went on. "You have to be prepared for it." He paused for a second. "I'm sorry to have to tell you this way, but Tai Babilonia tried to commit suicide last night. They're bound to ask you about it, it's all over the papers."

I felt as though I'd had all the air let out of me. Tai Babilonia, the 1979 World Pairs champion from California, was one of Michael's top clients. I knew her quite well and had been talking to her only a few days before.

"Oh, Michael, how awful," I said. "Is she going to be okay?"

"Yes, thank God," he said. "But she gave us a terrible scare."

"What do I say if they ask me about it?"

"I think you should just keep it simple, mention how

well-loved Tai is by many other skaters and that we are all rooting for her."

"Well, *I* certainly will be," I said. "Please tell her that I send my love."

Just as I was about to hang up, Michael said, "One last thing, Liz — tell Willy you understand about the 'Good Morning America' show."

I promised I would, and after I hung up I went back downstairs to find Willy.

"Well, I can't honestly say I'm happy about the arrangement," I told him, "but I'll do it. I know I don't have a choice."

"Welcome to the wonderful world of professional skating," Willy said.

The next day I rehearsed all day, until a taxi came to take me to the airport at 10:30 in the evening. I was weary and hungry, but we didn't have time to stop to get anything to eat.

I took a small plane to Minneapolis, then a larger jet to New York. When I arrived, a taxi took me to the hotel. By this time I was almost comatose. It was 2:45 in the morning.

An hour and a half later, at 4:15, the hotel desk rang to tell me that it was time to get up. I felt dreadful, sick to my stomach and light-headed. I just had time to shower, wash my hair, and put on makeup (which is difficult to do when your eyes are barely open), before another call let me know that an ABC limo was waiting for me.

When we arrived at the studio, I was taken to the greenroom for a few moments, then to the makeup room, then back for coffee and danish while I waited for the interview to begin. Finally they came for me and took me into the studio. I had no opportunity to talk to anyone beforehand. It seemed that the moment I sat down in my chair and the mike was attached to me, we were on the air.

Joan Lunden, the interviewer, introduced me as the Olympic silver medalist, and the star of the Ice Capades, which was about to open a new season in Duluth.

Her very first question, however, was the one Michael had foreseen.

"What was your reaction to the news of Tai Babilonia's suicide attempt?"

"I thought it was very sad," I replied. "I'm sure everyone who knows her is praying for her recovery."

She asked me some more questions about Tai, wished me luck in the show, and then we were off the air. That was it. It didn't seem worth all the effort it had taken to get me there. But everyone seemed to feel it had gone well. I was bundled into yet another taxi and rushed to the airport to catch the plane back to Minneapolis.

The plane sat on the runway at La Guardia for an hour and a half, waiting for permission to take off. When we finally got to Minneapolis, I had missed the connection to Duluth. I tried not to panic. "Okay," I said to myself, "now what do I do?" Then I remembered that Paul was supposed to drive from Minneapolis to Duluth that day and I called him, praying he hadn't already left. By some miracle, he hadn't, and I almost cried with relief.

"What on earth are you doing here?" he asked.

"I'll explain when I see you," I said. "But please could you pick me up and take me to Duluth with you?"

While I waited for him, I fought to stay calm. I was exhausted and stressed out, I hadn't had enough sleep, my routines in the show were under-rehearsed, and my foot was still a little fragile from the break. Now I was sitting in Minneapolis airport, having missed the plane. It was the thought of seeing Paul again that kept me from having hysterics.

I slept all the way to Duluth. We made it by 6:30, by which time nearly everyone in the show was frantic with worry. Michael was upset, and told me I should have let him know where I was. Apparently he had booked me on a later flight, but I never called him so he couldn't let me know.

I apologized for being thoughtless, and promised that it would never happen again. "I was just so tired and panicky that I couldn't think straight," I told Michael. "Please don't be mad at me."

I rushed to the dressing room. I had less than one hour to get ready and warm up. When I peered through the curtains, I saw that the arena was full. I knew my parents were there somewhere, and Paul too. I was nervous and keyed up, but I was looking forward to getting out on the ice.

The show went better than I could have expected. I missed a couple of cues, but nobody in the audience seemed to notice (though I probably gave the choreographer a small heart attack!). Afterward there was a party in the hotel. Tom Scallen came over to me. I hoped he had been pleased with my performance, but I couldn't tell from the expression on his face.

He stopped in front of me and looked me up and down. "You did a good job, Liz," he said. "It was a good show. But you have to lose ten pounds. You've gotten too heavy."

I was startled by this. I knew I had gained a few pounds, because of all the weeks off the ice. I was hardly a blimp, but on my small frame, 113 pounds looked like 130. I sighed. So much for the glamorous life of the ice-show star. It seemed to consist of no food, no sleep, and no fun.

My grumpiness didn't last long — I actually love skating in the Ice Capades, even the hassles of day-to-day touring, because I like the people I'm working with and I'm doing what I love best. But Willy was right about "the wonderful world of professional skating." Rule number one is that "the show must go on" — as an amateur, you can always withdraw from a competition if you don't feel up to it, but as a professional, you have to perform consistently and well night after night. Even one audience is too many to let down by not doing your best.

Rule number two is the one that Michael pointed out to me: publicity for the show is part of the job. Some weeks I would do as many as twenty-nine interviews. It got so that sometimes I couldn't think of a single thing to say, and that isn't like me at all. Or I'd forget what I'd said to whom, and either repeat myself or leave out something important.

The reporters I met were a mixed lot. Some were well-prepared and knew as much about skating as I did. But inevitably I got a few people who knew as much about skating as I know about basket weaving. I remember in Irvine, California, I agreed to tape an interview for a national television magazine program. I knew the interviewer had been sent a briefing sheet beforehand, so I expected she would at least ask the usual questions about the Olympics and the show.

When she arrived, she was dressed in a low-cut blouse and a leather miniskirt. She wobbled on to the ice in spike heels (it was a miracle that she didn't break an ankle) and stood there uncertainly, trying not to fall down. She turned to me and said, "Now, then, Miss Manley? What sport was it that you won the Olympic medal for?"

Since I was wearing skates and dressed in a skating costume, I couldn't believe my ears. So I turned to her, smiled sweetly, and said, "Bobsledding." I couldn't resist.

Reviewing ice shows is a fairly specialized field, and there are not very many reviewers who are skilled enough to be comfortable with it. All sorts of people are sent to cover the Ice Capades for the local media — sports journalists, dance critics, theater critics. I can understand that in some of the smaller centers, you're unlikely to find specialized skating reviewers. But I get really annoyed at journalists who review the show without having seen it. Ignorance is one thing, but dishonesty is quite another. What we need is some first-class writers who know the sport well and follow it intelligently. There are a few, but not enough to help raise the profile of skating in North America.

Chapter Twenty

The remainder of that first year's tour passed in a happy blur. I had never worked so hard in my life, flying ahead of the company each week to promote the show, and back again to skate the opening. I roomed with three of the other girls in the show, partly to save money and partly because I wanted someone to share things with. I liked it that way. Tom Scallen tried to tell me that it wasn't usual for the headliner to room with other skaters, but I wasn't concerned about tradition.

We were weighed in each week and if you were over your contracted weight, you could be fined. If you didn't lose weight, you could be fired. I weighed in with everyone else, even though I was told I didn't have to. But I wanted to be the same as everyone else, because we all worked together on the show and we all contributed to its success.

Far from gaining weight as we toured, I lost it. When

the tour reached Los Angeles, Peter and Sonya came to see the show. They came backstage afterward and Sonya said to me, "Elizabeth, you're much too thin. You need to gain some weight." It was a wonderful change to hear that, after all the years of being told I was too heavy. I got a real kick out of it!

I managed to pack a lot into that year in addition to the Ice Capades. In December 1988, I did my first television special, a variety show called "Dear Elizabeth," produced by Bernie Rothman for CTV. We taped the show partly in Los Angeles, while I was there on tour, and partly back in Ottawa. Christopher Plummer, Rich Little, Alan Thicke, Luc Robitaille, Barbara Underhill, and Paul Martini all took part. I enjoyed the change from doing the Ice Capades show, and learned a lot from working with such experienced television stars. Later I learned that the show had received the highest rating of any show on the CTV network that year.

I also skated in the World Cup competition for professional skaters in Ottawa and in the U.S. Open in Orlando that December and won both championships. It was a strange feeling to be back in competition again, and I found that I had missed some of the excitement of competing.

What I enjoyed most about my new status, however, was being invited to charity events. Sometimes these involved skating, such as the benefit I did for the Heart and Stroke Foundation, sometimes I had to take off my skates and pick up a baseball bat, as I did for the benefit that Wayne Gretzky organized to raise money for the CNIB, or the one that David Foster arranged in Victoria to provide money for children in need of transplants. I enjoyed these occasions, as they gave me a chance to meet new people, especially people from outside the skating world. Meeting them helped me keep a perspective on what I did. When you spend your life going back and forth from hotel to skating rink to hotel on tour, day after day after day, talking to people who don't skate is like a breath of fresh air.

Among the people I met were Prince Andrew and his wife, the Duchess of York. I had met her once before, when I had taken part in a benefit ice show in Cardiff, Wales. She had been the patron and she came out on to the ice after the show to talk to all those who had taken part. She asked me how I could do the things I did without getting dizzy, and mentioned that she was planning to go white-water rafting with Andrew in Canada. "I hope I don't drown," she said, laughing. "I'm terribly nervous about it."

I met them again at a reception given by the Governor General, Jeanne Sauvé. I was seated beside Prince Andrew at the luncheon and we talked about flying and the air force. Because my brother Tim had flown jets and helicopters, I was able to keep up my end of the conversation, and when we got up to leave, Prince Andrew turned to me and said, "Gosh — this has been fun."

In April 1989, I received the Order of Canada from Jeanne Sauvé. It was quite overwhelming to be honored in this way. I went through the ceremony in something of a daze, finding it difficult to believe that it was real. The experience of having a medal presented to me is a familiar one from skating, but this was not an award for skaters only. Not only was it an honor, but it reminded me that something was expected of me — I had to live up to it. I had to continue making a contribution to the country. It occurred to me that it must be less intimidating to receive the Order of Canada when your career is over, not when it is just beginning. It placed a certain responsibility on my shoulders, which was a little scary.

In July I participated in the opening of the Skydome in Toronto. It was raining hard outside, but they planned to open up the retractable roof anyway. I sat beside Tommy Hunter, wondering if the mechanism would actually work. It did, and sure enough, the rain poured in.

During the summer I was also invited to present the M.V.P. award at the NHL Hockey Awards ceremony with Gordie Howe. When the announcer referred to the two of us as "the legends of the ice from Canada," I was so surprised and flattered that I nearly dropped the award. We gave it to Wayne Gretzky. It seemed funny that I should be there, when it was my brothers who were the hockey players in the family. I know that any one of them would have given his eyeteeth to be in my place that night!

In July I co-hosted the Canada Day show from Parliament Hill in Ottawa with Roch Voisin. I am so used to performing on a rink looking up at the audience, that all these occasions when I stood on a stage looking down felt a little odd at first. I also had to learn not to take up too much space. I had been trained to cover the huge expanse of a rink, now I had to learn how to maneuver around lights and cables and microphones without tripping, and to stand on one spot for most of the evening. It took some getting used to.

❄

The second season of the Ice Capades was as enjoyable — and as jam-packed — as the first. I did another television special called "Hollywood Star Ice Review," although it was actually filmed in Whitby, Ontario, and Randy Gardner, Robin Cousins, John Curry, and Tai Babilonia (who had recovered very well by this time) all took part. I felt quite in awe of all the talent around me, but we found that we worked well together, and the whole experience was a lot of fun.

These were not the only legendary skaters I got to meet that year. I also got to present "Good Skate" awards to Barbara Ann Scott, Karen Magnussen, and Lynn Nightingale. These awards were created by the Ice Capades for community service and charity work.

I tried to follow in their footsteps with charity work of my own. World Vision of Canada sponsored a foster child for me — a three-year-old girl in Colombia — and I joined the board of directors of the Boys and Girls Clubs of Ottawa. I continued to act as National Spokesperson for the Canadian Mental Health Association and I also acted as a spokesperson for a newly formed group, the Starlight Foundation of Canada. This organization tries to fulfil the wishes of terminally ill children, a much-needed but heartbreaking task, working with children who have big dreams, but very little time.

In May, after the show was over, I taped a musical special for CBC in Toronto. It was called "Back to the Beanstalk" and I played Jack. Al Waxman, Jayne Eastwood, Heath Lambert, Sheila McCarthy, Tom Kneebone, and Ronnie Hawkins acted in it, and I got to skate with Robin Cousins, Joe Flaherty, Ben Gordon, and Harvey Atkins. The last three played three "chili beans." There was a number that involved all different kinds of beans — coffee beans, green beans, lima beans, jelly beans, chili beans — and when the production was over, the whole cast presented me with a hat that had one bean from each costume stitched on to it. Now all I need is the appropriate occasion to wear it!

❄

I have always liked to work hard and keep busy, and certainly my hectic schedule of touring and taping television specials and going to charity events gave me lots to do. But I learned a painful lesson about being *too* busy.

I had got to know Paul Hendrickson well during my first year of touring with the Ice Capades. We talked a lot on the telephone, and since he is the production manager for a company that stages concerts, sports events, political conventions, and theater presentations, he understood very well the types of stresses I was encountering, and the sort of life I led.

He managed to come and see a couple of my shows and at Christmas he came to Ottawa with his two daughters from a previous marriage, Jessica and Beth. Our families got along well, and I began to wonder if perhaps he was the right man for me. I confess to being a hopeless romantic, always dreaming of walking off into the sunset with Mr. Right — even though I told myself that in reality, the morning after I walked off into the sunset, I'd probably have to get up before dawn to fly off to do an interview somewhere and I'd probably never spend more than a few days in the same city as poor old Mr. Right.

Well, despite the difficulties of conducting a romance mostly at long distance, Paul and I grew very close, and in May 1989 he asked me to marry him. I was very much in love, longing for the kind of emotional stability that Paul represented in my life, and I accepted immediately. We planned a wedding for July 1990 and I began to make arrangements, enjoying all the details of sending out invitations, booking entertainment, having a dress designed — almost as if it were a skating show I was planning, not something that would make a huge difference to my lifestyle and future.

I was still madly busy all the time, of course, and the wedding plans made me even busier. What I didn't have time for was a good, honest look at my life and my career and a realistic view of just what kind of marriage Paul and I might have. From time to time I'd find myself wondering if I was doing the right thing, but before I had time to reconsider my plans, I'd be rushing off to do another show somewhere and pushing my doubts to the back of my mind.

A month before the wedding, I was in Los Angeles for a few days before going on to San Diego to do a show for Sea World. I had a few days to myself, with only Michael and Nancy there, and at last I started to take a long, hard look at what I was doing. It felt like the first time I had had a chance to think about my priorities since those lonely months after my breakdown in Lake Placid.

I thought about leaving Canada to live in Minneapolis with Paul. Moving away from Ottawa, from my family and friends, from the country that had been so good to me, began to seem very scary. I thought about my busy schedule and all the traveling I did, and I realized that Paul was going to get an absentee wife, which seemed very unfair to him. And I thought about the things I still wanted to achieve, with all the traveling and hard work they would involve, and suddenly I knew what I had to do.

I have made some tough decisions in my life: the decision to make a comeback after hitting bottom in Lake Placid, the decision to go to the Worlds after the 1988 Olympics. Those decisions were much easier to make, because I was really the only person affected. This time I knew my decision would hurt someone I cared for very much, and disappoint a great many other people. But I knew that the consequences of going through with a wedding when the marriage was likely to be subject to so many stresses would hurt everyone even more deeply in the long run.

Paul came down to see me in San Diego and we talked for a long time. Michael helped us sort out a lot of things, but really we had to work it out between the two of us. I felt awful about it, but I didn't back down. I believed that even if Paul didn't understand at first, one day he would know that I'd done the right thing by putting off the wedding.

✵

When this book was written, we planned to end it with the traditional "happy ending" — a wedding. Well, it still has a happy ending, but in the new version, I'm not walking down the aisle on my husband's arm, I'm standing on my own two feet and trying to be independent. I've got another season with the Ice Capades ahead of me, and after that, who knows? Whatever it turns out to be, it will be something I choose for myself. I now know that I can't make decisions in a rush for emotional reasons, and that I can't please everyone all the time.

I look back and I can see that the road to where I am now was bumpy and full of pitfalls. At times I wanted to quit, at one point I actually *did* quit, but something always made me put my skates back on and give it another try. One of the things I still want to accomplish is to find a way to help other young skaters who get into difficulties — financial, emotional, or physical. I wouldn't want anyone else to have to go through some of the problems I went through. On the other hand, if I hadn't had those problems, I might not have developed the will to overcome them, the will to succeed. So I can honestly say that in spite of all the setbacks I encountered, in spite of the times when I didn't know how I was going to continue, I really wouldn't have wanted to have it any other way.

Acknowledgements

Elva Clairmont Oglanby and I would like to thank everyone who was involved in the development and production of this book. In particular, we thank Denise Schon, publisher of Macmillan of Canada, for her initial interest and enthusiasm. Also Donna Williams, freelance copyeditor, who helped to make the book more readable. Finally, we thank Philippa Campsie, editor-in-chief of Macmillan, who was unfailingly supportive and cooperative during the editorial and production process and who helped to give the book its final shape.